GLOBAL HISTORY OF THE PRESENT
Series editor | Nicholas Guyatt

In the Global History of the Present series, historians address the upheavals in world history since 1989, as we have lurched from the Cold War to the War on Terror. Each book considers the unique story of an individual country or region, refuting grandiose claims of 'the end of history', and linking local narratives to international developments.

Lively and accessible, these books are ideal introductions to the contemporary politics and history of a diverse range of countries. By bringing a historical perspective to recent debates and events, from democracy and terrorism to nationalism and globalization, the series challenges assumptions about the past and the present.

Published

Thabit A. J. Abdullah, *Dictatorship, Imperialism and Chaos: Iraq since 1989*

Timothy Cheek, *Living with Reform: China since 1989*

Alexander S. Dawson, *First World Dreams: Mexico since 1989*

Padraic Kenney, *The Burdens of Freedom: Eastern Europe since 1989*

Stephen Lovell, *Destination in Doubt: Russia since 1989*

Forthcoming

Alejandra Bronfman, *On the Move: The Caribbean since 1989*

James D. Le Sueur, *Between Terror and Democracy: Algeria since 1989*

Mark LeVine, *Impossible Peace: Israel/Palestine since 1989*

Hyung Gu Lynn, *Bipolar Orders: The Two Koreas since 1989*

Nivedita Menon and Aditya Nigam, *Power and Contestation: India since 1989*

Helena Pohlandt-McCormick, *What Have We Done? South Africa since 1989*

Nicholas Guyatt is assistant professor of history at Simon Fraser University i

About the author

Timothy Cheek holds the Louis Cha Chair
of Chinese Research in the Institute of Asian
Research at the University of British Columbia.
He is also editor of the journal, *Pacific Affairs*.
His research, teaching and translating focus on
the recent history of China, especially the role of
Chinese intellectuals in the twentieth century and
the history of the Chinese Communist Party. His
books include *Mao Zedong and China's Revolu-
tions* (2002) and *Propaganda and Culture in Mao's
China* (1997), as well as *New Perspectives on State
Socialism in China* (1997), with Tony Saich, and
The Secret Speeches of Chairman Mao (1989) with
Roderick MacFarquhar and Eugene Wu.

Living with Reform: China since 1989

Timothy Cheek

Fernwood Publishing
NOVA SCOTIA

Zed Books
LONDON | NEW YORK

Living with Reform: China since 1989 was first published in 2006

Published in Canada by Fernwood Publishing Ltd, 32 Oceanvista Lane, Site 2A, Box 5, Black Point, Nova Scotia BOJ 1BO
<www.fernwoodbooks.ca>

Published in the rest of the world by Zed Books Ltd, 7 Cynthia Street, London N1 9JF, UK and Room 400, 175 Fifth Avenue, New York, NY 10010, USA
<www.zedbooks.co.uk>

Cover designed by Andrew Corbett
Set in OurTypeArnhem and Futura Bold by Ewan Smith, London
Index <ed.emery@britishlibrary.net>
Printed and bound in Malta by Gutenberg Press Ltd

Distributed in the USA exclusively by Palgrave Macmillan, a division of St Martin's Press, LLC, 175 Fifth Avenue, New York, NY 10010.

A catalogue record for this book is available from the British Library.
US CIP data are available from the Library of Congress.

Library and Archives Canada Cataloguing in Publication
Cheek, Timothy
    Living with Reform : China since 1989 / Timothy Cheek.
Includes bibliographical references and index.
ISBN 1-55266-207-1
    1. China--History--1978-2002. 2. China--History--2002-. I. Title.
DS779.4.C43 2006   951.059   C2006-902639-4

ISBN 1 84277 722 X | 978 1 84277 722 0 hb
ISBN 1 84277 723 8 | 978 1 84277 723 7 pb

Contents

Acknowledgments

I would like to thank Nick Guyatt, the general editor for Zed Books' Global History of the Present series, not only for drafting me into this project but also for his steadfast editorial support and shockingly extensive (and extremely useful) commentary on the first draft. My heartfelt thanks, as well, to the editors at Zed Books, particularly Ellen McKinlay, for their patience and encouragement. I am grateful for additional comments from the external reviewer, as well as from John Friedmann, Guo Xiaolin, David Kelly, Michael Schoenhals, James Spear, and Jeffrey Wasserstrom. This book is dedicated to Song Jin for advice, example, and encouragement, but mostly for reminding me how much I have yet to learn.

T.C., Vancouver
July 2006

Chronology

ventures; sets up Special Economic Zones; decollectivizes farmland; Hu Yaobang becomes General Secretary and Zhao Ziyang becomes premier; leadership division over direction of reforms; Hu Yaobang resigns and top intellectuals purged, January 1987

1989   Student protests in Tiananmen, April–May, and military repression on 4 June; Jiang Zemin replaces reformist leader Zhao Ziyang; Berlin Wall falls

1990s   Popular patriotism education drive; Mao fever; growth of Falungong; reforms resume 1992 with Deng Xiaoping's 'Southern Tour' and confirmed at 14th Party Congress, October 1992; double-digit GDP growth for most of the decade

1994   Huai river runs black from pollution; its water not fit to drink for the rest of decade

1999   US planes bomb Chinese embassy, Belgrade, Yugoslavia

2001   September 11 attacks in USA; George W. Bush visits Shanghai and China joins 'War on Terror,' October; China joins WTO, November

2002   16th Party Congress, where Hu Jintao becomes General Secretary

2003   Wen Jiabao becomes Premier at 10th National People's Congress, March; Three Gorges Dam first stage completed; HIV-Aids scandal and SARS scare

2006   National People's Congress stresses 'harmonious society' and rejects private property law

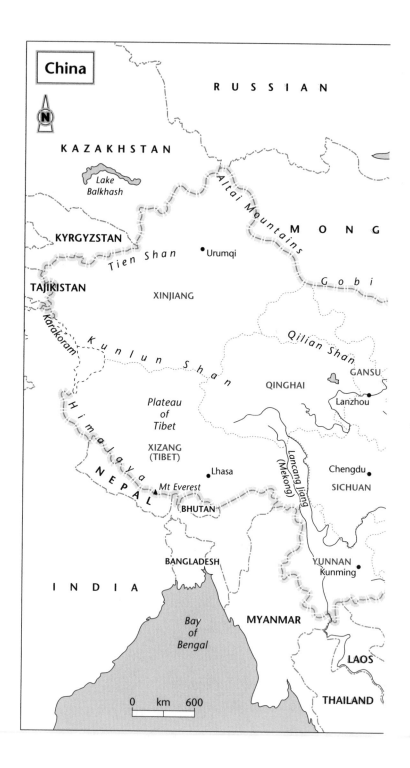

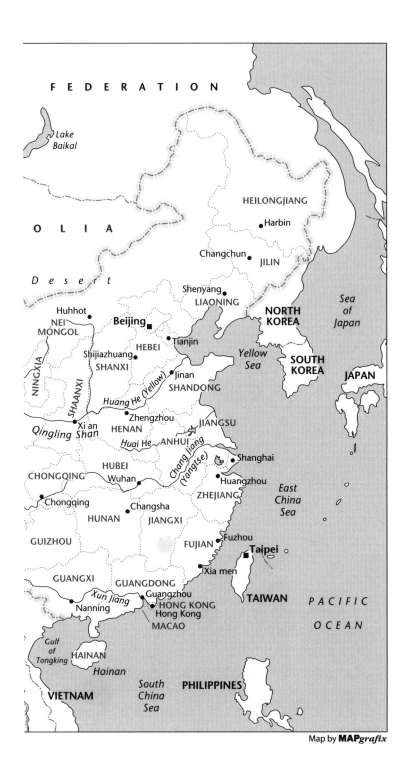

Map by **MAP***grafix*

Preface: what does Tiananmen mean?

China is huge. For those who study it, it dominates our understanding of Asia and revolves as a giant planet in the international solar system; for those who do not, it is an immense gap – of 20 per cent of global population – in their understanding of our world. Yet China remains a great mystery to most people, and it regularly surprises specialists. Worse, it is an oriental screen of flat images and prejudices that dangerously pass as knowledge of the world's largest nation, the People's Republic of China (PRC), and ancestral home of over 100 million overseas Chinese who engage with their culture in its current nation-state.

Everyone knows that China is a major force in the world today, but what do we need to know about China? We know that China is a socialist state undergoing profound reform. This reform includes moving a planned economy to a market economy and globalizing China's commerce, media, and culture. Is China going to become more like us? More like Europe or the USA? If that is the case, then why is China not democratizing along with the states of eastern Europe since 1989? How do we understand the plain fact that China has not democratized but has nonetheless developed economically at a tremendous rate over the past two decades – faster than any other major country in the world? What do all these changes mean for China, the world, for you and me?

I approach these questions by offering you, the reader, a map of how China works today and an account of how it came to be this way. It is my hope that you can use this map to discover your own informed opinions. This is neither a general history of China nor a political essay. It is an invitation to make China part of your life, not least because it is a shaping force of your world. The problems China faces are the problems we all face; how various Chinese address these problems will profoundly influence our world. This history, then, is an introduction to a relationship, an introduction based on my experience in researching and teaching about China for some thirty years. While I provide citations for important details in my narrative or to acknowledge the work of others upon which I have particularly relied, this book is not documented in the full academic fashion. Interested readers are invited to consult the Suggested Reading section (p. 163) for an initial listing of well-written collections and studies that will take them farther into China and the extensive scholarship on it.

It is impossible to write or read history without expectations, assumptions, and preferences. So we begin with the fundamental challenge of good historiography: awareness of expectations – *What are various Chinese expectations? What are international, and especially US, expectations and assumptions about China? Most immediately, what are our assumptions and expectations about China?*

Picturing China: seeing beyond Tiananmen

The most enduring contemporary image of China for most people outside China is Tiananmen and the solitary man blocking a column of tanks. In the spring of 1989 massive student demonstrations in this politically sacred central square of Beijing appeared to paralyze the government and certainly garnered the attention of the world. The demonstrations seemed to be about democracy, the students were brash and exciting, the sheer scope of the demonstrations – hundreds of thousands of people in the square for weeks – all raised hopes of international observers that China was on the brink of a new day. The brutal military crackdown that occurred on 4 June 1989, killing what we then thought were thousands, dashed the hopes of all and ushered in a harsh campaign against the protestors.[1] International reaction was swift and strong. Condemnation was nearly universal, led by the unlikely team of the USA and France. The enduring image referred to above comes from the crackdown: the lone man in front of the column of tanks. Resistance to oppression! The little man against the state. China once again had dashed our hopes.

The image and realities of Tiananmen warrant revisiting. It is not simply an unfortunate affair of the past among many. It remains a centrally defining issue not only for international commentators (led by Europhone intellectuals including South Asian elites) but lives on as an unresolved tension in contemporary PRC politics. If we look at Tiananmen again we can bring to the surface the expectations and assumptions that shape and often bedevil our understanding of China today and which drive various Chinese experiences. We will be catching glimpses Tiananmen throughout our story and will return to it at the end. By then we shall have seen that even though the events of Tiananmen suggest that 1989 changed China as surely as it transformed Russia or eastern Europe, the narrative of Chinese reform does not arrange itself so neatly. More important for life in China today are the consolidation of reform in 1992 and the living Maoism which continues to define social habits and expectations, as well as political possibilities and limitations.

Tiananmen remains a useful touchstone for exposing anyone's expectations and assumptions about China, as well as their preferred politics. For Westerners it has always been about democracy, but for most Chinese it has been about the unfinished promises of reform.

Democracy now! International perceptions of the 1989 Tiananmen demonstrations and repression were shaped by two international forces. The first was technical and contingent, the second was ideological. For the first time global TV was present in downtown Beijing with the permission of the Chinese government. The world saw its favorite TV news anchor or reporters doing live feeds from the heart of China. The TV crews were not there to cover the student demonstrations. That was unintended. The authorities invited international media to Beijing in the spring of 1989 to cover the historic visit of the General Secretary of the CPSU, Mikhail Gorbachev, on 15 May. This was a vastly important rapprochement between the two alienated leaders of the world socialist movement. No Russian leader had visited China since Khrushchev in 1959, and the two countries had fought a perilous border war in 1969. Deng Xiaoping and the CCP leadership were eager to show their new accomplishments after a decade of economic reform and opening to international contact and trade. They also wanted to bring to a close this unhappy chapter in their history and to settle a key arena of their foreign relations. To promote this goal, the Chinese government invited international media, and especially the TV networks, to set up shop in Beijing for Gorbachev's visit.

But then unstoppable student demonstrations walked onto this carefully prepared stage, ruining the whole diplomatic effect. Why the students did this and why the CCP was unable to enforce its efforts to stop them remained unclear to these visiting observers. But quickly they picked up and focused on an ideological term – democracy. The students clearly were protesting. But protesting against what? Hu Yaobang was clearly an issue. The former CCP leader had died on 15 April 1989 after two years of disgrace following his purge for being too liberal. The marches to Tiananmen began, then, as public demonstrations of affection for Hu Yaobang at the time of his official funeral. Chinese politics is obscure, but student banners and placards quickly made a compelling point: democracy. And, for the benefit of the TV cameras, English versions of this key slogan (*minzhu*, 民主 in Chinese) appeared: Democracy. Could these be democracy advocates challenging the dictatorial communist rulers of China? It was a news story too good to be true. Not only student leaders but even the international China experts in Beijing at the time said yes – these are pro-democracy demonstrations. The TV announcers enthused, the specialists explained the tentative nature of this democracy movement, but we all hoped that this would become the start of a democratic transition in China. Perhaps China would lead the socialist world in making 'communism with a human face' a reality, creating a truly democratic socialist order. The labour agitations in Poland and popular demonstrations in Czechoslovakia, plus rumblings in East Germany, suggested in that heady spring that the world was ripe for a change. The Berlin Wall might still be up and the Soviet Union still the other superpower, but Gorbachev had started a change. Could it be, would it be, China that would take the giant step first?

Love China–hate China These expectations and assumptions led both the general media and the scholarly community to underestimate the dangers facing the demonstrators. We were stunned by the brutal and effective repression of the popular demonstrations. More to the point, we were furious. In our reactions to Tiananmen and the military repression of the demonstrations scholars joined the general public and political leaders in blaming and punishing China for dashing our unrealistic expectations. We shifted from great hopes for China to great anger. These responses reflect ill-informed and extreme images of China that dominated Western media, and much academic work, over most of the twentieth century. The simplest way to test those reactions – and our reactions to the issue of Tiananmen today – is to ask: what is your reaction to Burma? Many more explicitly pro-democracy demonstrators were gunned down on the streets of Rangoon in August 1988, but Dan Rather or the BBC were not doing live feeds on that.[2] In straight quantitative terms of killings the Burma repression in 1988 was far greater than China's in 1989, but scholarly and popular, and most importantly diplomatic, reaction was far more muted. Media matter. But more so, the image of China in our minds matters. Burma is one of many failed states where such repression is shamefully common. China bears the brunt of our hopes and endures the fury of our vexed expectations.

This Dr Jekyll and Mr Hyde image of China in the Western mind is not new, but it is obviously distorting our understanding of China today. Harold Isaacs captured this schizophrenic view of China in his 1958 book *Scratches on Our Mind*.[3] China, as well as India, served as a screen onto which Americans projected their hopes and fears. Richard Madsen has updated that insight from a sociological perspective. A co-author of Robert Bellah's famous study of American values, *Habits of the Heart*, Madsen argues that all public discussion in the USA, and most influential scholarship, about China has been animated by the role of China as a 'secondary common reference point' – that China studies served as a metaphor for public debates over the meaning of American democracy and identity. The tension in that identity, according to Madsen, is the contrast between two contradictory versions of being American – individualistic and communitarian. China's communist revolution during the cold war served as a way to argue about this tension inside American society by arguing about freedom and socialism in China. In the 1980s, the promising reforms and reopening of China to Western nations encouraged Americans to think that the tensions between individual opportunity and community equity could be resolved, that unleashing the power of free enterprise would inevitably create democracy. 'Tiananmen smashed this comforting illusion,' wrote Madsen; '[it] dramatically demonstrated that the creation of a market economy did not inevitably bring democratic community.'[4] Even worse, it has now become clear that China's continuing spectacular economic growth has rested in part on the repression of public protests and increasingly unsavory working conditions for millions of workers. When I raise China's role as a proxy metaphor for local political debates with my European colleagues, I find their experience in Britain, Germany, France, and other nations parallels the picture presented by Madsen. The best way to release China from this proxy role is first of all to learn more about the complexities of life in China and of the hopes and concerns of various Chinese.[5]

Unfinished business If international and Western impressions of Tiananmen are seriously distorted by our own concerns, then what does Tiananmen mean to Chinese? The first thought is to say 'the Chinese'. But there is no single Chinese representative to ask. As we will see in Chapter 1, China is both huge and internally diverse. We have to separate out key actors in Chinese society – at a minimum, the government, the protestors, urban Chinese, and rural Chinese. Yet while their concerns and views on Tiananmen vary, one theme ties the diversity of Chinese views on Tiananmen: unfinished business. Tiananmen serves as a reminder to people across China of the unfinished business of reform, of the promises of development with equity that have yet to be fulfilled.

Beginning with Deng Xiaoping, who led the military repression of protestors on 4 June 1989, China's leaders have denounced the demonstrations in and around Tiananmen as a 'counter-revolutionary disturbance.' That remains the official verdict to this day, and even the new generation of top leaders in power today who were not directly associated with the suppression show no signs of reversing this decision. It has been nearly two decades; one shouldn't expect a change in official views any time soon. This is because the fundamental concerns of government leaders remain: they fear *luan*, chaos. To them the students marching in the streets of Beijing, disobeying direct government orders, mocking the police and even People's Liberation Army (PLA) soldiers, were a terrifying image not of democracy but of the chaos of Red Guard gangs in the Cultural Revolution. Deng Xiaoping and his associates had all been tormented by the Red Guards and had seen what they felt to be ordered and good government shattered by such popular demonstrations in the 1960s. They felt they had to protect China from any repetition of the unfairness of the Cultural Revolution. This is the image the Chinese Communist Party (CCP) gives of the Tiananmen demonstrations in public defenses of the repression – 'we brought order when street hooligans were terrorizing Beijing.'

This is not the view of the student leaders and over a million participants in the 1989 Tiananmen demonstrations. They were first and foremost demonstrating against *corruption* among political leaders and for more job opportunities. A decade of reform since 1978 had brought two profound social changes that upset students, workers, and urban residents in general. First was the end of the state-run job appointment system. Until the late 1980s students and trainee workers were guaranteed employment, even if they did not have the freedom to choose employers. The opening of the job market was experienced not only as an increase in the freedom to choose but also as a loss of job security. Second, economic reform had brought inflation to urban residents on a fixed income. The lightning rod for these fears and frustrations was official corruption. Students, in particular, chafed at seeing mediocre classmates get plum jobs or coveted overseas graduate fellowships because they were family members of high officials. Tiananmen started as a funeral march for Hu Yaobang but became an outlet for these fears and frustrations. Democracy was only a general term for fairness and equity, not a specific call for a multiparty electoral system. Indeed, the students were quite elitist. Workers wanted to join the demonstrations, but China's top university students did not want to associate with workers. In retrospect, the chance for a Chinese Solidarity Movement was missed.[6]

Urban residents supported the student demonstrations enthusiastically. White-collar workers, industrial workers, service workers, civil servants, and pensioners all shared the frustrations and fears about job insecurity and inflation in the face of official corruption. In a sense, the government was right to fear the legacy of the Cultural Revolution, because here was a generation that knew it was possible to attack the government on the grounds of fairness and equity. While ordinary Beijing residents no more wanted the street fighting and political turmoil of the Cultural Revolution years than did government leaders, they wanted change and sought ways to support the students non-violently. That is why most of the public support for the demonstrators by urban residents was aimed at providing food and water for the hundreds of thousands of daily demonstrators and later in blocking the advance of military units. The relation between urban residents, including workers, and the demonstrating students was partially traditional: public respect for scholars ran deep. Both the Confucian tradition and the more recent May Fourth tradition (from an earlier patriotic demonstration in Beijing in 1919 – then against Europeans for cutting China out of the Versailles Treaty) gave students the role as representatives of the public good. This was a role eagerly accepted by the students and widely acknowledged by urban residents. They expected students to help call on the government to fulfill the promises of reform.

Rural residents were not impressed. The corruption that urban residents saw as a sign of bureaucratic abuse, rural residents saw as typically urban. Like urban residents and university students, people in the suburban villages and townships, as well as rural communities across China, also experienced the new insecurities and inequities that came with reform. In the early 1980s rural areas, particularly in the densely populated eastern and coastal provinces, did very well as the reintroduction of private farming brought new income into agriculturalists' hands. But continuing price reform in the mid-1980s had increased the cost of fertilizer and decreased the price of farm produce, cutting into those profits. To rural residents this appeared to be another case of abuse of power by 'the cities.' On top of this resentment, the behavior of the demonstrating students upset many rural Chinese. It was unpatriotic to shame China on TV – TVs that had only recently come into villages and farming homes across China in the 1980s. Even during the heady days of May 1989, when the Chinese media gave fairly neutral coverage of the demonstrations, it looked to rural Chinese like *luan* – chaos. Images of boys and girls dancing and touching in public, being rude to police, and clogging up the streets gave the impression that these were decadent, chaotic, and unpatriotic people who richly deserved to be slapped down.

There is one last significant group of Chinese to note when it comes to Tiananmen – those who were not born yet, or were very young. These are the youth, university students, and young professionals of China's middle class, as well as young farmers and migrant workers. For them, Tiananmen is history; they are much more concerned with the contemporary realities of reform – their own education and training, jobs, and entertainments. This generation knows almost nothing about Tiananmen, because public discussion is taboo. Their lives are built around cell phones and brand names or sweatshops and migrant labour camps. They have no reason to think of Tiananmen today. Indeed, China has a profound generation gap. The living Maoism that shapes their parents' generation is only weakly represented in this generation – for better or for worse.

Living with reform: what is fair and who decides?

Today Tiananmen remains a touchy issue in China. There are recurrent calls, particularly behind closed doors within the CCP system, to re-evaluate the event and its participants and to remove the 'counter-revolutionary disturbance' verdict placed on it. This is not merely a Western obsession. Loose talk about the Tiananmen protests (along with 'Free Tibet' and 'Falungong') on the Chinese Internet and blogs will get you into trouble even today. Tiananmen is a ticking time bomb in Chinese political culture, but more as a symbol for the lack of political reform today than as an example of the sins of the past. As we look at China in this book, Tiananmen will be with us always as a warning to double-check our assumptions and expectations, as well as those of our informants. It can also serve us as a metaphor for the unresolved tensions experienced by Chinese of various social classes and cultural groups after a quarter-century of great economic and some political reform. Living with reform has challenged Chinese of all walks of life to confront the problems of development – distribution of wealth, distribution of the burdens of economic upheaval, distribution of the costs of pollution, distribution of opportunities for work, housing, the good things in life. Living with reform boils down to the immensely complex politics of the issue that was at the heart of Tiananmen: what is fair and who decides?

To address these issues, this book offers the contemporary history of China thematically. The first chapter describes the physical, social, and political realities of what is more of a continent than a country. It gives a snapshot of how China works today and sets us up to explore in the following chapters: how did it get to be this way? And what is it like to live in this world? Chapter 2 turns to the living history of Maoism, in the form of both the still-ruling CCP and the continuing life-ways that have resulted from the conscious and unintended consequences of the Maoist system of 1949–76 and, especially, from the trauma of the Cultural Revolution decade (1966–76). These are the language and the formative experiences that shape living with reform in China today. Chapter 3 looks at the intentions, actual events, and preliminary results of post-Mao reforms (1976–92). This bridges the Tiananmen affair of 1989 because, as we shall see, the actual performance of reform does not fit easily with the master script that focuses on 1989 in the world. For both the government and most people in China it was events in 1992 which have made the biggest difference in how their lives play out today. Chapter 4 gives a social history of the operation of Deng Xiaoping's model of reform: economic reform and openness without full political reform up to the present. Here we will glimpse something of the *experience* of various Chinese actors and meet the unintended consequences of reform. In particular we will see why the forces for democracy are so weak in Chinese society. Chapter 5 looks at the later portion of the same period (in the new century) to view the social and political *reactions* to the consequences of reform – neo-Maoism, popular nationalism, severe if uncoordinated criticism of local government corruption, intellectual ferment over how to promote social justice along with economic growth, international worry over 'rising China.' Finally, Chapter 6 turns our focus to China's role in the world and, of course, its primary international relationship with the United States. This chapter brings our narrative round full circle to suggest how the information gleaned from the core chapters can help us to see beyond, or through, Tiananmen and to form a more accurate and useful understanding of what China is doing and what that means for us.

1 | Making sense: what is 'China'?

China is more a continent than a country. In terms of geography, population, and ethnic diversity, China corresponds to no other country on the planet other than India. It is simply vast, with a wide range of geographic areas, an immense population, and a dizzying variety of ethnic communities and identities. While the modern state of India corresponds in many ways to the geographic and ethnic diversity of China, it does not carry China's long heritage of political unity or recent experience as a Leninist state.[1] What, then, is China? In our preface we noted that it is not helpful to think of 'the Chinese' as a unitary group. How shall we look at the land, the people, the society, and the political entity we call 'China'?

If China were placed over the northwest corner of Eurasia, it would stretch from Dublin to Damascus and from Moscow to Marrakesh: hugely different physiographic regions with independent sub-histories. We have to ask: why is it one country and not at least a half-dozen? A first answer is history. One way to make sense of this tension between geographic diversity and political unity in China is to imagine that the Roman Empire had recovered from Germanic attacks and reconstituted itself as an effective, stable, and powerful regime in the sixth century CE, comprising the lands not only of Augustus's empire but what became the Byzantine Empire – all under the central control of Rome – and that this Roman Empire lasted (with Mongol invasions and interregnums) until 1912. History matters, but it does not predetermine current choices. Life in the social, economic, and political systems that define the People's Republic of China (PRC) knits a diverse range of people together and makes the 'idea of China' real and compelling to them despite immense differences in their personal circumstances.

This is a fundamental dialectic in Chinese life and thought today: the contrast between the *unity* of 'China' widely felt by the majority

Han population (not to mention the government) and the actual physical, economic, and social *diversity* of life in the PRC and among 'Cultural China' (Hong Kong, Taiwan, and more than 100 million Chinese in Southeast Asia and across the world). The purpose of the chapter is to suggest how we can make sense of these forces of integration and diversity by focusing on *how the system works* and contrasting how different major social actors *experience their place* in that system. Thus we move from geography, to demography, to economic activity, to political order.

If we are to understand how living with reform in China today operates and what it means for those in it (as well as for those of us outside China), then we must understand some of these basic facts of life, of social order and experience. We need this detail to begin to answer the questions of reform: why does privatization look so different to workers in northeast China and farmers in southwest China? Why do some women complain that life since the end of Mao's rule is worse, while other women cheer the changes of the past three decades? Is the CCP getting stronger or weaker? The context of China's systems will help us answer these questions.

China's systems

Like any polity, China is built on land, climate, people and their social organizations, economic activity, and political order. Within these systems different groups and individuals have a wide range of experiences and thus divergent interests. It is this complex, but functioning, set of systems which organizes life in China today.

The land China's land mass is about equal to that of the United States: 9.6 million square kilometers, and only slightly smaller than Europe's 10.15 million.[2] China's population, however, clocking in at 1.26 billion in the 2000 census, is four times greater that the USA's at slightly less than 300 million and well over twice the size of Europe's population of some 480 million. One in every five persons on the planet lives in China. This huge population is not spread evenly over the area of the PRC. Population density for China as a whole is 622 persons per square kilometer, but rises to three times that (1,800/sq. km) in the eastern coastal regions and falls to a tenth of that (60/sq.

km) in the western regions.³ And, as one would expect in an area the size of Europe, geography and climate vary widely across China, contributing to different local economics and lifeways.

Geographic China can be envisioned in two parts, north to south, and three layers, east to west. The biggest divide in China is the separation of warm, wet, rice-growing south China and hot/cold, dry, wheat-growing north China. In the south, wet-rice agriculture defines the landscape with flooded paddy fields and the intensive cultivation of two and in the far south three crops of rice a year. Temperatures are moderate and rain fairly regular. In the north, the land looks yellow from the dominant soil, loess, the wind- and water-borne soil from the northwest that gives the Yellow River its eponymous colour. The weather is more continental with freezing winters and hot, dry summers. Rains are not reliable enough to sustain wet-field agriculture, so dry farming of wheat, barley, and other grains predominates. One simple and obvious difference in lifeways that stems from the geographical and climatic differences between north and south China is that traditionally southerners eat rice more often, while northerners claim noodles and breads as their traditional fare.⁴

In the western regions this separation is erased by altitude. The three layers of China from west to east begin with the Tibet/Qinghai plateau, which lies some 4,000 meters above sea level and occupies fully 20 percent of China's landmass. This huge western region is sparsely populated and is home to several non-Chinese 'minorities' (i.e. peoples that claim the area as their own, such as the Tibetans, but which count as minorities in the PRC). Radiating out from this plateau are the major rivers of China, as well as of South and Southeast Asia: the Yangzi, the Yellow, the Mekong, the Red, the Ganges, and the Brahmaputra. Moving east from the Tibet/Qinghai plateau there is a series of lower plateaus descending to the major plains of coastal China, in particular the North China plain that runs from Beijing to nearly the Yangzi, and the Northeast or Manchurian plain (in the provinces just north of Korea). Population density increases as one goes east and to lower altitudes. Land in China thus ranges from sea-level plains to alpine parks, from zero to 4,000 meters. On the globe it stretches from 50 degrees north to under 20 degrees, with Guangzhou, the capital of Guangdong province, as well as Hong Kong, and Hainan Island in the tropics, while winter lows in China's northeast regularly reach minus 25–30 degrees Centigrade.

Accounts of China's geography usually feel compelled to explain China's international isolation (a product of the cold war) by invoking the name in Chinese for China: *zhongguo*, the Middle Kingdom. Historical research has long since shown that the geography of China – with high mountains to the west and big oceans to the east, dry deserts to the north, and impenetrable jungles to the south – no more inhibited trade and contact with eastern and Southeast Asia than did mountains, rivers, and deserts in Europe and North Africa. Established trade routes across the Siberian steppe, through the Tarim basin, down the Red River into what is now Vietnam, and especially on the 'Southern Seas' operated throughout Chinese history.[5] Famous examples include Chinese military expeditions well into Central Asia, as well as continuing trade along those routes extending to India, Persia, and the Mediterranean, during the Han Dynasty (205 BC–220 CE), the Tang (618–907), the Yuan (1279–1368), and the Qing (1644–1912). Of course, the last two examples were Chinese governments run by non-Chinese, the Mongols of the Yuan and the Manchus of the Qing. This only emphasizes the connections between China and its neighbors.

Yet the image of a 'closed China' lurking behind the Great Wall remains. This comes from European experience with China in the Early Modern period and from the anomaly of the Ming Dynasty (1368–1644). When Europeans arrived in some numbers and with official patronage in the sixteenth century, they came to trade and to convert. For the next two hundred years Europe was the suitor and China the not very interested 'prize.'[6] China was better ruled, more prosperous, and the producer of goods wanted by European traders (porcelain, silk, tea, and, of all things, rhubarb). For Jesuit priests and a range of European merchants, and ultimately British diplomats at the end of the eighteenth century, it was a case of frustration as the two different diplomatic and economic systems failed to connect in the way the Europeans wished. The talisman of this friction is the mission of Lord Macartney in 1793. This was part of a quasi-diplomatic effort on the part of the British East India

Company to the Qianlong Emperor in Beijing. The mission, its hundred-plus members, and the array of British manufactures and technology were viewed as 'tribute from England' under the Chinese diplomatic system of the day. Macartney's efforts to get China to act like a Westphalian European nation-state, and thereby to grant Britain a diplomatic mission in Beijing, were dismissed by the Qing state out of hand.[7] Things did not change until Britain was able to project sufficient military power to force the Qing to accede to their demands. This they did in 1842. By that time China was decidedly not better ruled and no longer able to defend itself against new military technologies from Europe. Political corruption associated with dynastic decline and dramatic population growth in China combined fatefully with industrialization and imperialism in Britain to create a reversal of fortunes. The Opium War – over Chinese efforts to limit British opium imports – saw the military defeat of the Qing forces and the diplomatic subordination of Chinese foreign affairs to the norms of civilization in what we today call the period of high European imperialism.

This history – rather than geography – has left two enduring impressions. For Europeans, the negative views of frustrated opium traders and imperialists have become general: China is weak, corrupt, doesn't want to be modern, and actively tries not to engage with the civilized world, yet, as Adam Smith famously opined, China represented the golden, nearly boundless market for European manufactures. For the Chinese, the outraged confusion of the Qing elite endures: the West is predatory, violent, self-righteous, and uninterested in Confucian civilization, but it is fearsomely powerful and brings some wonderful technologies. These ambivalent feelings on both sides endure, to be engaged or enflamed as contemporary events prompt, but they come from historical experience and not geographic or cultural determinism.

People and local society What geography and climate have contributed to Chinese life is internal diversity. People living in different ecological zones naturally have different foods, farming, and other activities. In addition, across this range of geographic and climatic areas are spread some fifty-five different ethnicities. China and 'the

Chinese' are not uniform. The two biggest realities of ethnicity in China are, first, that there are nearly 100 million members of minorities who feel themselves to be meaningfully different from the Han majority, and second, the Han majority really is an overwhelming majority – comprising nearly 90 percent of the population of China. [8] Unlike in Russia, the dominant ethnicity, in China's case the Han, is not threatened with demographic submersion under the numbers of non-dominant ethnic groups. Indeed, the problem, as we shall see, runs the other way: various minority areas, particularly in Tibet and Xinjiang, run the real risk of being swallowed up by Han in-migration. They face not 'ethnic cleansing' but 'ethnic drowning.'

Yet the dominance of the Han is not a uniform experience. There is a wide diversity among the Han, based not only on region and economic class, but on dialect and local identity. The net result is what Susan Blum has aptly described as 'China's pluralism,' built around three axes: ethnic diversity, cultural diversity based on general lifeways, foodways, and language, and diversity of religious expression.[9] These three building blocks – ethnicity, local cultural identities, and religious practices – are the foundation of personal identity and community experience in China. They create identity but also difference. One of the challenges for the PRC is how to embrace this de facto social and cultural pluralism and the differential experiences and responses of different ethnicities, localities, and religious communities, since this social diversity structures the experience of living with reform in China.

China's minority populations are vibrant human communities and many have links with neighboring countries, such as the Uighurs in the west, Koreans in the northeast and groups that cross China's borders with Southeast Asia.[10] Additionally, minority populations are predominantly spread along the border regions of China – including a quarter of China's total land area in the thinly populated western regions of Tibet, Qinghai, and Xinjiang. In all, the territories that are largely inhabited by minority groups account for over half the entire area of the PRC. Thus, for China as a whole, these minority populations and where they live connect to three critically important issues for China today: border issues and national security, natural resources for development, and 'room to live' for the overcrowded Han populations in eastern China.

The Chinese government has put a great deal of effort into its minority policies, including special arrangements and affirmative action, as well as repression of threatening ethnic organizations or demonstrations. The PRC has established five provincial-level autonomous regions in areas where minorities have traditionally been majorities and in which these groups are meant to have political leadership at the local level. Of China's twenty-eight provincial-level units, the five autonomous regions designed for ethnic minorities are: Inner Mongolia, Xinjiang Uighur, Ningxia Hui, Guangxi Zhuang, and Tibet (see map). Autonomous administrative districts for minorities extend down the governmental chain to thirty-one autonomous prefectures and ninety-six autonomous counties in other provinces. In these areas, for example, government work may be done in both the locally designated minority language, as well as in Mandarin Chinese. Generally, the Party and government leadership in these areas includes many of the relevant ethnic groups, and quite often there are special subsidies or other preferential policies to help what are usually rural and poor communities of minorities.[11] As we will see under political organization, below, autonomous does not mean independent.

A brief look at a few of the fifty-five ethnic groups gives a sense of China's astonishing pluralism on the ground. The largest ethnic group is, of course, the Han. With well over a billion people, its customs are China's official customs, as is its language. As we shall see below, there is considerable sub-ethnic diversity in language and customs among the Han. The largest of the minorities is the Zhuang, with nearly 16 million. Most Zhuang live in the southwest province of Guangxi and are related to people across the border in Vietnam. The odd thing about the Zhuang is that by the 1950s they had assimilated to a considerable extent with Han culture when the new PRC state encouraged them to pay more attention to their own cultural characteristics![12] The Guangxi autonomous region was established for them in 1958, very likely as a trial run for the establishment in 1965 of China's last and most controversial autonomous region, Tibet.

Muslim or Hui identity makes up ten of the fifty-five recognized ethnicities (Hui, Uighur, Kazakh, Tatar, Tajik, Uzbek, Kyrghyz, Dongxiang, Salar, Bonan). They total about 17 million people and speak a range of languages from Indo-European to Turkic/Altaic to Chinese. Two of China's autonomous regions – Xinjiang and Ningxia – are dominated by these Muslim communities. The Uighurs alone are the fifth-largest ethnic group in China, with a population of about 7 million. Uighur separatist groups have been staging violent incidents in recent years in Xinjiang and militating for closer ties with other Turkic-speaking Muslims in Kazakhstan, Kyrghyzstan, and Tajikistan.[13] The Uighurs in Xinjiang are a prime example of the political-economic-security issues of minorities in China. The government is deeply anxious about Islamic militancy, claiming that Uighur agitation is none other than 'Islamic terrorism.' Xinjiang has many valuable minerals and natural resources, and finally, Xinjiang has space. Han in-migration into the area has been immense in recent years, bringing the local majority of Uighurs to a minority percentage of the population – a classic example of 'ethnic drowning.'

The Hui are the third-largest single minority group in China. At about 8.7 million, they live all around China, predominantly in the cities. Hui are mostly Chinese-speaking and often intermarry with Han. In some cities the only marked public difference is that Hui, as Muslims, don't eat pork – the favorite meat of the Han. In other areas, Hui have experienced tensions with other ethnic groups. For example, in Western Sichuan province the Hui have moved into the Songpan district to handle local commerce in recent years, displacing the local Tibetans, who resent the change.[14] Ethnic tensions can be between minorities as well as with the dominant Han.

Ethnic tensions and racism are real in China. The key conflict is between the dominant Han of eastern China and the local minorities. The prejudices of ordinary Han against many minorities are conflated with class differences; as well, many minorities live in impoverished rural communities. These problems are not new, and were the subject of comment from both Sun Yat-sen, founder of the Chinese republic in the early twentieth century, and Mao Zedong in the 1950s. Sometimes, however, the social tensions are between different minorities, particularly in border regions where Han are rarely seen. In some areas of Yunnan province, in the southwest, members of the Bai or Miao groups are more likely to complain about the way the Yi control the administrative networks for minorities in the province. They suspect the that Yi are passing on government largesse disproportionately to their own group.[15]

Linguistic diversity and regional identities are the key forms of Chinese pluralism. While 70 percent of the population speak Mandarin Chinese (*Putonghua*) as their native tongue, the other 30 percent or some 360 million people speak other dialects at home. Leaving aside the Thai, Turkic, and other non-Chinese languages, the major dialects of the Chinese language can be as different as English and German. Beijing natives, who speak Mandarin, cannot understand the *yue* dialect of Guangdong (commonly known in the West as Cantonese). So, too, with the *minnan* dialect of Fujian and the *wu* dialect of Shanghai, or the Hakka dialect spread in small groups across South China. As with all languages, shared spoken language builds a sense of commonality, and different speaking marks different identity groups. Unlike with fully different languages, however, the same Beijingers who cannot understand a spoken conversation between Cantonese speakers can understand the same conversation if it is written in normal Chinese characters. It is for this reason that there can be national newspapers in China that any literate reader of Chinese can read regardless of which dialect they use to pronounce the words. Indeed, this characteristic of Chinese – diverse and mutually incomprehensible speech but shared written language – helps to define both the diversity and the unity of China. Language thus provides one answer to the question posed by this chapter: how to account for China's unity in spite of its actual diversity.

With language comes regional or local identity. Provincial stereotypes are strong in China – of course, more in terms of other provinces than one's own: Sichuanese are sly and tricky, Hunanese are quick-tempered, Guangdong people are interested only in business. Despite marked improvements in telecommunications and travel, and a huge migrant population, most Chinese, in fact, do not travel far and rather spend most of their lives in their native district. In the south, local identity is also tied to clan or lineage organization. Many villages in South China have been until very recently single-surname villages, all Wangs or Zhaos or Lims. These lineages are community corporations that own the land, the temples, and the other assets that define daily life. Here family and local organizations blend quickly into what Westerners call religion.

Religion in China officially comprises five recognized organized religions: Buddhism, Daoism, Islam, and two forms of Christianity – Catholicism and Protestantism. There are somewhere between 70 and 100 million practicing Buddhists and educated guesses are that there are about 250 million practicing Daoists (or participants in Daoist-oriented popular religious practices). About 17 million self-identify as Muslims. Catholics claim 10 to 12 million adherents, and various Protestants estimate between 25 and 35 million believers.[16] Counting Chinese Christians is particularly difficult because many adherents belong to the illegal house church movement. After the CCP came to power in 1949 Christian churches, like other social organizations, were required to become Party-run organizations. Many Christians refused and so went underground. In the reform period the Christian churches are increasingly accepted, but any sign of organized unofficial churches brings state repression.[17] While international attention has focused on Chinese Christians, most Chinese who participate in organized religion do so as Buddhists or Daoists. Numerically, most Chinese do not participate in organized religion beyond the social and cultural practices of local temples, festivals, and customary rituals associated with unorganized popular cults or local worthies.[18]

The Party's fear of unofficial organizations, such as Christian house churches, drives the most famous case of religious persecution in China: the Falungong. As we will see in Chapter 5, this syncretic religious sect frightened the Party in 1999 by its show of organizational strength through a surprisingly large demonstration in front of the Party headquarters at Zhongnanhai in Beijing, and this has prompted the banning of the sect and persecution of its members.[19] Falungong is, however, but one example of a much broader, but not centrally organized, form of Chinese spiritual practice – qigong. Visitors to China often comment on morning exercisers in the urban parks doing t'ai chi or other qigong exercises. This is a popular national pastime and has philosophical aspects that some would call religious, though qigong research institutes study these exercises from a scientific perspective. Qigong and the well-known practice of feng shui – the science of optimal placement according to geomantic principles – form a shared cultural-religious practice across classes and regions in China. While most qigong practice in China is health-oriented and personal – much like yoga in the West – it has become part of the new cybersects in China, which revive traditional religious secret societies via the Internet, and of which Falungong is but the most notable example.[20]

Most of everyday life in rural China has a religious aspect in terms of local tutelary gods, spirits, local temples, and community festivals. These religious activities are usually related to a Daoist or Buddhist temple, but do not rigorously follow one of the major institutionalized religions. Tony Saich gives a telling story of village life where clan, religion, and the Party mix in unexpected ways:

> In one mountain village, I witnessed the performance of a traditional ceremony to welcome a young man into adulthood. At the entrance to the village I was met by a middle-aged man who introduced himself as the local Party secretary and he guided me to where the performance would take place before exiting. Shortly, the ritual began with an elaborate demonstration ... led by a man draped in a tiger skin and wearing a crucifix and who occasionally slipped into a language that no one could understand.

With a shock, Saich recognized the man in the tiger skin as none other than the Party secretary he had just met, and also that the strange language included many Latin words. He later learned there had once been a Jesuit mission in the village.[21]

It is important to remember, however, that this story is just about as strange to middle-class professional and other urban Chinese in Shanghai or other major cities. It has become part of the major geographical split in China today: rural and urban. That difference is predominantly economic – poverty in rural areas that are not near the major cities (and thus able to benefit from market opportunities) drives most of the cultural differences and certainly shapes the image urban Chinese hold of rural areas as 'uncultured' or 'backward.' It is a fundamental fact of life in China today that while almost 200 million people now are or aspire realistically to middle-class life, and so engage in the globalized commercial consumer economy that makes Shanghai and Guangzhou look so exciting, at the same time, at the other end of the spectrum, some 200 million live in dire poverty and a total of almost 500 million are poor by any definition.

One divide cuts across all ethnicities, regions, and class: *gender*. It will come up time and time again in our story – reform has, in the main, been better for men than for women. China is still very much a patriarchal society and the status of women, while changing and improving, particularly for the middle classes in urban China, is not only not improving relative to the Mao period for rural women but getting worse.[22] A toxic mixture of traditional habits, global objectification of women as advertising sex objects, and an unintended result of affirmative-action policies in state-owned industries (in which maternity-leave policies and other supports for women encourage newly independent managers to cut female staff first) threatens to poison Chinese society.[23] Much of this is driven by economics.

Economic activity Under Mao, China was a state socialist society with a centrally planned economy. There was no private property, beyond limited personal effects. Factories, farms, and financial institutions all belonged to the state or the collective. Since the late 1950s an important part of China's political economy has been the household registration system, or the *hukou*. This system of internal passports essentially locked peasants into rural communities and inhibited the migration of rural laborers to the cities, as has happened in all other developing economies. The *hukou* system was introduced at about the time that rural landholdings were collectivized into communes.[24] Thus, from the 1960s all workers in China – whether in agriculture, industry, or services – had their place in this public economy. Either one was a rural resident in a commune or one had an urban *hukou* and worked in a state-owned enterprise or work unit (*danwei*). The work unit was a 'full service' employer. If one's work unit was a bank, then that bank would provide highly subsidized housing for its employees – usually in apartment buildings built right next to the work area – arrange for healthcare, education for the children, and provide the ration coupons valid for that district (it was these ration coupons which helped keep unauthorized outsiders from moving to a city). One was usually assigned that job at the end of high school or college and generally one stayed at the same job throughout one's career.[25] Indeed, in some industries it became the norm that one of an employee's children could succeed to the parent's job. In Mao's China work life was built around such urban work units or rural communes.

The *hukou* and *danwei* systems have slowly unraveled in reform China. By the early 2000s some 150 million rural workers had migrated to urban areas for temporary or long-term work, all without *hukou* permits, but because ration coupons have been phased out and social services – from housing to education – have been put on the market, if one has the money one can live in the city. More so if one is willing to live in a shanty and to endure the risk of arbitrary detention and deportation – then one can work in the city and send money home.[26] Internal remittances from these rural-to-urban migrants, we shall see, are a key part of the national economy in China today. The biggest change in a generation in China has been the creation and boom of the residential real estate market. There simply wasn't one in 1984, but twenty years later most urban residents own or rent their apartments and a very few own luxurious villas in gated communities. Life in reform China has broken the world of the work unit and commune – for better and for worse.

Economic organization in China today is increasingly capitalist or, in the parlance of the CCP, following the rules of market socialism. This has brought stunning economic growth and painful economic disparities. China has developed, and annual GNP growth rates of 10 percent are real and reflect greater wealth and productivity in Chinese society, but these gains are not distributed equitably and come at considerable cost in terms of environmental sustainability and social order. What these changes have done to China's systems can be summarized as follows. More people now work in industry and service sectors than in agriculture. Smaller cities and large market towns are increasingly connected to urban centers and, indeed, begin to look indistinguishable from suburbs of big cities. These smaller cities have many of the major commercial, and even some international, shops and banks; international films and censored international TV are available just about everywhere. Market gardens near cities, specialized crop production in counties with good transport to cities, increased resource extraction of coal, timber, or herbs from mountain districts – all contribute to this vibrant but largely uncoordinated economy.

The results, as we shall see, have changed the lives of nearly every person, even though they might not leave their local community or meet an outsider throughout their whole lives. For some, life is fantastically better; for many it is somewhat better; for still far too many it is worse than twenty or thirty years ago. Economic change has wrought new divisions in Chinese society. The first is between the urban and the rural. While this split is not new, it is far more acute than before. One reason is the feminization of agriculture. Many villages are nearly without young and middle-aged men, who have gone off to the cities to earn money. Farming is left to the women, who must also handle childcare and care for elders. Between villages and small cities are thousands of joint-venture factories – the places where all those things in Wal-Mart are made. These capitalist enterprises bring some of the worst – sweatshop – conditions of international business into the heart of the countryside. Finally, those men (and some women and families) who have left the countryside have become the 150-million-plus 'floating population' that does the construction and menial labour in China's cities. At the same time, the decommissioning or privatization of the state-owned factories has put tens of millions of Chinese industrial laborers on the street – either as officially unemployed or disguised as *xiagang*, 'off duty.' Many of these changes stem from China's most recent reforms, made to enable its membership in the WTO.[27]

The impact on community life and personal identity of these massive economic changes from 'the plan' to 'the market' for people all across China drives the life under reform that we will see in the rest of this book. This is a volatile and unstable brew of opportunity, anxiety, and suffering. And it spreads across a continental landmass and a billion and a quarter people. The Chinese Communist Party has to try to keep order over this diverse society and to try to guide

China in its integration with the world economy. Like any government, it does this to stay in power and to maintain the perquisites of its membership.

Political order The PRC is an anomaly in political theory. It is a socialist state, led by a one-party Leninist regime that still claims Marxism-Leninism-Mao Zedong Thought as its ideology. But it is a capitalist economy with many of the features of the capitalist market seen in non-socialist societies under the contemporary influence of globalization. Most political theories predict that a market economy should lead to political democracy. While this might be the case in the long term, it is not certain, and market reform certainly has not brought an end to the CCP's autocratic rule in China. The primary question for China is not when will it democratize, but rather can the CCP or any government handle the challenges of reform and deliver a reasonably prosperous, stable, sustainable, and equitable life for the people of China.

The press and popular accounts talk glibly about 'the Party.' But what is the political system in China? Two systems rule China: the state government of the People's Republic and the Chinese Communist Party. The state is organized by the central government in Beijing represented by the National People's Congress and State Council. The non-central government is comprised of twenty-three provinces (including Taiwan, which is not under PRC control), five provincial-level autonomous regions for ethnic minorities, four municipalities directly under the central government (Beijing, Tianjin, Shanghai, and Chongqing), and two Special Administrative Regions (SARs), Hong Kong and Macao (see map). Below these provincial-level units are two main levels of government: counties or cities and, at the bottom level, townships. Villages are below the formal level of government. From the bottom up, China's hundreds of thousands of villages and 96,000 townships are part of some 2,400 counties, which are parts of twenty-eight provinces.[28] The provinces deal with the central government. Villages have elected officials. Officials at higher levels are appointed by the *nomenklatura* civil service system under the State Council. So, townships have appointed officials, cities have mayors, provinces have governors.

Yet this picture does not explain how governing works in China. At every level there is the Communist Party, most notably in the form of Party committees and the all-powerful First Party Secretary of those committees at each level – village, township, county, city, province. Thus, administration in China runs on two tracks, the government department track and the Party track.[29] Officially, the Party 'supervises' the administrative work of the government department, but in fact the Party officials set the rules and objectives, albeit in consultation with state officials. We can look at the organization charts for the government – the State Council, central ministries, and provincial administrations – and at the various levels of the CCP separately, but in fact they always work in tandem. The state administration is staffed by about 37 million cadres or about 3 percent of the population. The CCP has some 68 million cadres, or some 5 percent of the population (of course, almost all of the state cadres are CCP members). Thus the Party-State employs 5 percent of the population. Given the interpenetration of state organs and Party committees in the Chinese Party-State, it is more useful to look at *scale* to understand this aspect of the stage that is China – Beijing, the provinces, and the localities.

The central government in Beijing is the State Council and the approximately forty-five ministries (such as Education, Foreign Affairs, National Defense, etc.) and commissions (such as the State Development Planning Commission) under it. This is the executive branch of the Chinese government. Its leaders are appointed by the National People's Congress (NPC), China's legislature, whose members are delegates elected by lower-level (provincial) People's Congresses and by the armed forces. This is a very indirect form of democracy that does not include general elections among the citizenry. The real power, however, resides not in this state administration but in the committees and organizations of the central CCP. There is also a congress system in the Party. The National Party Congress of about two thousand delegates meets every five years (the 16th Party Congress met in 2002, the 17th will meet in 2007) and elects a Central Committee (CC) of about two hundred members that meets annually. The CC in turn elects a politburo of about twenty members and a standing committee of less than a dozen (as well as a secretariat chosen from among these to handle documents). This politburo and its standing committee are the centres of power in China: here all the major decisions are made. The leaders of these organs are the names we hear as the leaders of China: Jiang Zemin, General Secretary and leader of the politburo until 2002, and Hu Jintao, who holds those positions now.

At the provincial level a similar pattern of People's Congresses and Party Congresses, with attendant administrative councils and bureaucracies, is evident. The most important aspect of provincial administration is the relative independence of Party and government leaders at the provincial level which has emerged under reform. Under Mao, Beijing ruled both in policies sent down and revenue sent up under the central plan. Reform has brought decentralization. While the central government still exerts political control through its right to review and sanction appointments of leading provincial personnel (in the *nomenklatura* system), its fiscal capacity and prestige have waned. State revenues have declined from 36 percent of GDP in 1978 to approximately 15 percent today. Beijing has less to offer provincial leaders, who must face the social and economic problems in their regions pretty much on their own. Thus, behind the façade of the communist state exists a very real diversity of interests and dispersal of real political power between the three levels of government – central, regional, and local.

At the local level the pattern is repeated: a similar model of Party-State and a similar relation, this time between the provincial and county authorities and between county and township authorities. The reality of political organization in China today is a dangerous combination of too little democracy in terms of citizen control of local governments and too much latitude for local leaders. The result has been bad administration from wasted development projects to downright oppression. It is precisely to begin to address this emerging social anomie at the local level that the central CCP has sanctioned real popular elections of village officials (non-state jobs below the township level that nonetheless affect local households) while at the same time reintroducing and reviving Party cells in local government and organizations.

The reality of this festering problem with corrupt local states across China is captured in the language of rural residents throughout China. When they speak of the state, they use two different words. When the say *zhengfu*, they mean the local state, and they are usually complaining about the poor administration or corruption found there; when they say *guojia* they mean Beijing, the leaders of the central government whom they trust and believe have their best interests in mind, and to whom they look for help.[30] This brings to mind civil rights activists and local blacks in the USA, who looked to the federal government in the 1960s to help them fight racist policies in their particular state. One of the most pressing challenges facing the CCP leadership today is just this: can the central government make good on these popular hopes? Can the *guojia* enforce reasonable policies on China's out-of-control local *zhengfu*? It is clear that Hu Jintao and his premier, Wen Jiabao, are trying to do this; it is by no means clear that they will succeed.

Diversity of experience in China's system

People and communities experience the changes of reform in China to a large degree according to their place in the geographic, demographic, economic, and political systems that make up 'China.' A few images will serve not only to illustrate what Susan Blum calls China's pluralism but also to show how the systems we have introduced in this chapter operate and both affect and are used by various people across the PRC. At this point, it is my hope that these examples will raise more questions in your mind than answers, answers I hope to suggest in the chapters to follow.

- Uighur youth and men in Kashgar, Xinjiang, listening to underground cassette tapes of Central Asian music and political satire; they feel very little connection to China and a great deal of anger toward the Han.
- Tibetans, Hui, and Han fighting over resources in northwest Sichuan – in this case the Tibetan herders are more angry at the new Hui middlemen than at the Han representatives of the state.
- A poor farming family in Hubei forced to move to higher and rougher ground to make way for the Three Gorges Dam; now they cannot make ends meet; their son goes to Tibet for a better-paying job.

- Han tourists soaking up the sun and fun in Xixuangbana, in southernmost Yunnan province, where cross-border drug and sex trade has made the region a hot spot for HIV-Aids.
- Destitute laid-off workers in Liaoning province, in China's northeast 'rust belt,' hit the streets to demonstrate against what they view as a corrupt local administration. Despite threats from riot police, they refuse to go home.
- Chinese yuppies sipping lattes at Starbucks in Beijing, while migrant laborers swarm on the bamboo scaffolding of a new office building being constructed across the street.
- A middle-aged farm wife scrabbling out a life while feeding three children and caring for her husband's aged parents while he is in Guangzhou trying to earn money as an itinerant laborer.

How can we make sense of this disparate collection of lives? Shared historical experience is the connecting thread of these people's lives and, to some degree, of their thinking. While their contemporary experiences diverge widely, they share a common living heritage: Maoism.

2 | Living history: what was Maoism?

China is a socialist state. The popular story in the Western press about the demise of communism worldwide ignores the plain fact that the largest country in the world is still ruled by the same Communist Party that came to power in Stalin's time. The Berlin Wall may have fallen, the two Germanys may be reunited, the USSR only a memory and eastern Europe part of the neo-liberal world order of capitalist markets and democratic elections, but China remains the stunning exception to this story. China's government is not elected. The CCP continues to rule both in name and in fact. There are some 68 million card-carrying Communist Party members in China, most in positions of responsibility. And yet China is obviously successful, as measured in GNP, international influence, and arms build-up. It is a force to contend with. In the narrative of 'the end of history' put forward by Francis Fukuyama and others in the 1990s, communism was supposed to implode and give way to liberal democracy and unrestrained markets. China's recent rise, while still led by a communist party, challenges the neo-liberal story of market and democracy.

China is, however, a capitalist economy. If there is irony for advocates of the demise of socialist states, there is more irony for advocates of socialism. China's Communist Party has overseen the massive restructuring of the political economy of China from the planned economy of state socialism to a market economy over the past twenty-five years, beginning in the early 1980s. What sort of capitalist system remains to be seen, as it is not associated with liberal democratic practices of parliamentary democracy, broad-based elections, or an independent judiciary able to enforce decisions. Yet there is private property, a housing market, labor mobility, international-style banking, some stock markets, and, of course, China's membership of the WTO. This capitalism, called 'socialism with Chinese characteristics' by the CCP, is fraught with problems, with giddy winners and miserable losers and with dangerously unsustainable patterns of energy and land use that could well leave China unable to grow enough food or keep the lights on in the not so distant future. Does this capitalism under a communist party mean that the ideology of revolution, Maoism, is dead?

These contrasting realities – a socialist state and a capitalist economy – bump up against each other in daily life in China. Contemporary Chinese society is itself framed by two systems. The first is the physical and human geography that we met in the previous chapter – the stunning diversity that exists under the hegemonic belief that there is a unitary China (shared by most of the population as well as asserted by the political leadership). The realities and rules of local culture, kinship, patriarchy, and personal networks shape the experience and expectations of each member of this diverse population that calls itself Chinese. The forms that these diverse norms and practices take today, however, have been fundamentally shaped by one common experience: Maoism.

Living Maoism is the second system that frames social life in the People's Republic of China today. It is the mental world shared across vast differences of city and village, rich and poor, Han and minority, man and woman, young and old. Each distinct person and social group brings its own meanings to this mental world, and contributes to its transformation, but the tools they use to support the Party, ignore it or oppose it are the ideas, assumptions, and habits of Maoism.

Maoism is an ongoing dynamic in contemporary China. Officially, Maoism is the writings and ideas of Mao Zedong, the undisputed leader of the CCP since the 1940s and the founding leader of the People's Republic until his death in 1976. It is properly known as 'Marxism-Leninism-Mao Zedong Thought,' and remains the official ideology of both the CCP and the constitution of the PRC. All government policies, and much cultural and academic work, as well as formal laws and regulations, explicitly invoke this ideology. It is the public doctrine of China.

Over the past fifty years political Maoism has created both social practices and profound habits of thought. These two things – official

Maoist ideology and the social life of state socialism with its enduring habits of thought (assumptions, values, ways of reasoning)
– comprise the living history of Maoism. That living history shapes
the production of reform policies by the state leadership, the application of those policies by local government and business leaders,
and the experience of these reforms in practice by ordinary people
in China. The operation of this living history of Maoism is quite
complex, and often surprising. The official ideology is no longer
widely believed. Cynicism about Party pronouncements is rife. Yet
it defines the field of public debate, if only by providing the terms
of reference. Party intellectuals, reformers of various stripes, and
even dissidents all avail themselves of the language, ideas, and terms
found in Mao's Thought to debate public policy. The social structures of state socialism and the lifeways they produced continue to
influence life on the ground even as those structures are changed.
The residential passport system (*hukou*) and the work unit system
(*danwei*) still shape capitalist enterprises even as the harsher aspects
of these two systems have been abandoned to be replaced by the
insecurities and inequalities of the market. Most fundamentally, the
habits of thought and practices of public life that emerged under
'actually existing Maoism,' particularly in the destructive Cultural
Revolution decade of 1966–76, shape the expectations and ways
of making a point among most people in China.[1] Residual respect
for intellectuals and the expectation that it is up to the state to fix
things combine with intolerant modes of argument and illiberal
public demonstrations to shape the writings and activities even of
democracy advocates.

Maoism has this living history quite simply because China's political leaders and those in their forties and older *lived* under the
Maoist system. The lessons they learned from that history shape the
expectations they have brought to reform. They pass these habits
and expectations on to younger generations by social modeling.
The young, however, have a different take on the lessons of Maoism
– from utter materialism to renewed social radicalism. Yet we can
only make sense of these young people, as well as their elders, by
understanding the conversation with Maoism that informs their
response to living with reform.

This chapter begins with an introduction to what Mao Zedong himself thought about Chinese society and development. What is the *content* of Maoist ideology that people today appear to remember? In the second half we will look at the role Maoism still plays in China three decades after his death – as the orthodoxy of the government (what is said) and as the orthopraxy of ordinary citizens (what is done). This chapter is not an intellectual history of Maoism from 1949, nor is it a political history of Party reform policy in the 1980s (we will turn to those reforms in the next chapter). Here we want to paint in brief compass the main parts of living Maoism, its key points up to 1976 and an introduction to how Maoism is experienced in China today.

Maoist history: remembering the revolution

Lenin famously remarked that revolution has to begin from current realities. What were the 'current realities' when China entered its current reform in the late 1970s? What did the recent history of Mao's revolution mean to leaders and ordinary people when he died in 1976? What are the lessons that various people in China have drawn from that revolutionary history? Clearly those 'lessons' have changed over the past thirty years (and we will leave the details of the context of the 1970s and 1980s for the initiation of these reforms to the next chapter), but some themes have remained throughout that also bring to mind to the case of the Soviet Union and the reforms under Gorbachev:[2] Maoism was socialist, patriotic, and committed to progress. It was also chiliastic, led to political repression and economic disaster, and yet was widely believed well into the 1970s. It is still a force to contend with as China's leaders have sought to find a new legitimacy among its citizens. Similarly, socialism as a way of life is central to contemporary China, as it is to the states of the former Soviet empire, including the socialist status hierarchy, a muscular police and security system, and a resulting reluctance among most people to confront the government directly.

Historians have long noted that Mao Zedong, the man, was not only deeply flawed but also was not the all-powerful creator of the People's Republic of China or even of the CCP; that real history is, naturally, much more complex than the leadership of one man.[3] Yet he was, and remains, the most charismatic and significant leader of twentieth-century China and both the official source of legitimacy for the CCP and a powerful model of rebellion for generations of Chinese. The key point to keep in mind about the power of Mao today is this contradictory legacy.

This enduring contradiction in Maoism can be summed up in two phrases: 'leave it up to the Party' and 'it's right to rebel.' The first reflects the considerable prestige of the CCP associated with its role in China's turbulent twentieth-century history. Even though various people in China today dismiss the extreme claims of revolutionary correctness or question the gaps in official Party histories, the CCP is broadly credited with saving China from imperialism, warlords, and poverty. For many in China, the greatest achievement of the CCP, for which Mao is the embodiment, is the establishment of the Chinese nation-state and the restoration of order in 1949. The many sins committed by Mao and the CCP since then have not – yet – utterly overshadowed this singular achievement.

China's modern history is marked by a few dates that trace more than a century of humiliation at the hands of foreigners, particularly the British and the Japanese, which was ended by the revolution led by the CCP and Mao. It begins with the Opium War of 1840–42 that forced China to accept at gunpoint European rules of diplomacy and trade, as well as British sales of opium in China. Depredations by European and American imperialists continued through the century as domestic order under the Qing Dynasty slipped away and China suffered a terrible civil war, the Taiping Rebellion, which raged from 1850 to 1864 and killed some 25 million people.[4] In 1895, to add insult to injury, China's former tributary state, Japan, sank China's 'modern' northern fleet and inflicted a humiliating treaty that marked the beginning of fifty years of violent Japanese imperialism on the Asia mainland. Things went from bad to worse as the Qing wobbled and then toppled in 1911, the new Republic of China quickly unraveled into competing warlords, and the two most energetic modern political parties (the Nationalist Party or Guomindang, GMD, and the CCP) – both modeled on the Leninist Bolshevik party and supported by the USSR – fought a long civil war from the late 1920s until 1949. In the middle of this Japan invaded China as part of what we know as World War II and the Chinese remember as the Anti-Japanese War (1937–45). Throughout all this, rural and urban misery increased, and literate Chinese truly wondered whether 'China' was doomed to collapse as a polity and disappear as a culture. Mao did not create the revolution that would avert that disaster, but he did come to represent the solution. He captured the mission of the CCP powerfully in his 1940 essay, 'On New Democracy,' and that project still resonates in China today:

> Since the invasion of foreign capitalism and the gradual growth
> of capitalist elements in Chinese society, that is, during the hun-
> dred years from the Opium War until the Sino-Japanese War, the
> country has changed by degrees into a colonial, semi-colonial, and
> semi-feudal society. China today is colonial in the enemy-occupied
> areas and basically semi-colonial in the non-occupied areas, and
> it is predominantly feudal in both. ... It is precisely against these
> predominant political, economic, and cultural forms that our revo-
> lution is directed.[5]

Mao captured the success of that revolution in 1949, standing on the balcony of Tiananmen and officially declaring the founding of the People's Republic of China on 1 October. Just a few days before then Mao coined a phrase that has stuck: 'the Chinese people have stood up!' That claim has endured, as the PRC has endured and now prospers under the rule of the CCP. On the basis of this success the CCP maintains that in important public matters it is best to 'leave it up to the Party.'

But the rule of the CCP has not been smooth and Mao, the na-tional hero, is also the culprit of two decades of massive suffering from the mid-1950s until his death. This is the other side of the Maoist coin: it is right to rebel. Three campaigns stand out in this sorry history which squandered so much of the political capital of the founding of the PRC and caused in excess of 20 million needless deaths between 1959 and 1969. These campaigns and the losses they brought the CCP and China are an equal part of Mao's legacy today, of which most Chinese are now well aware. Yet despite the failure of these political campaigns – and in part because of experience in them – Mao's call to resist bureaucratic tyranny and to fight for the rights of the dispossessed still inspires some in China today. Mao's call that 'it's right to rebel' particularly speaks to those who have lost out under reform.

The first of Mao's 'it's right to rebel' campaigns was the Hundred Flowers Campaign and the associated Anti-Rightist Campaign. The former began in 1956, but came to a climax in May 1957, and the latter took off that June and ran well into 1959. The Hundred Flowers was Mao's response to the Soviet thaw and to the reality of bureaucratic oppression under state socialism in general and in China in particular. He believed the intellectuals of China had been 're-educated' away from their bourgeois and colonial roots to a socialist view of the world and that they could usefully criticize the CCP in public in order to correct the faults of Party rule and so bring the Party to a new and higher level of 'revolutionary success' in 'serving the people.' It was heady stuff, especially coming from China's revered supreme leader – it was OK to criticize the Party! Mao's Party colleagues were not enthusiastic; they believed China's intellectuals were still bourgeois and could not be trusted to comment on, much less publicly criticize, the vanguard of the proletariat. Mao insisted and the results, in a thrilling and surprising month of public debate in May 1957, fully confirmed the fears of the Party faithful: the intellectuals did not suggest tactical improvements to Party rule but rather demanded strategic political change and even the institution of multiparty politics and democratic elections.

Mao and the Party closed ranks, stopped the criticism, and launched a punitive campaign to eradicate such 'Rightists' from China's ranks of intellectuals and cadres (since a number of loyal CCP members had also taken the invitation to offer various suggestions for improvement). In the Anti-Rightist Campaign it did not matter if you had denounced Mao, suggested democracy, or merely wondered whether your local Party secretary was putting his hand in the till, all critics – and many who had made no criticism at all – were denounced and punished, with thousands sent to labour camps.[6] China's professional classes – inside and outside the Party – were cowed into silence and submission.

The intellectuals having proved unequal to the task of 'continuing the revolution,' Mao turned from politics to the economy and put his faith in the rural masses. In spring 1958 he pronounced an ambitious economic development campaign, the Great Leap Forward, designed to propel China from semi-feudalism, over the stage of capitalism, directly to the stage of advanced industrial socialism and, very quickly, to the nirvana of communism. Mao's unrealistic enthusiasm combined with a slavishly loyal Party bureaucracy and a silenced professional class to produce the most organized and planned disaster in China's history. Insane agricultural production targets produced famine by diverting labor from a mixed economy to imagined super-yield fields of rice that, in the end, did not produce, and to ill-designed irrigation projects.[7] At the same time, labor, material, and industrial output were wasted on 'backyard furnaces' intended to produce steel in a decentralized and 'self-reliant' manner similar to CCP village economies during World War II. These furnaces produced only slag and wasted yet more labor. The heart of the disaster was the willingness of local Party leaders to pretend in order to please Mao and the compliance of central leaders who were afraid to stop the madness. The ensuing famine from 1959 to 1961 is the greatest single disaster in the history of the PRC and rivals the entire Japanese invasion in the scope of human suffering. Far more Chinese died under the CCP in a time of peace than during the Sino-Japanese War.[8]

The disaster of the Great Leap Forward shook the CCP to its roots, and yet the Party did not collapse. It rebounded, and tried to learn from the mistake. Most of the Party returned to orthodox, technocratic Leninist methods of industrialization and social control. While the collectivized communes of the Leap were maintained in name, control of farming was more or less returned to the household; engineers, scientists, and other educated Chinese were brought back from detention and/or honoured as they were asked to fix the economy.[9] The leadership set out to modernize China step by step under what the premier, Zhou Enlai, suggested in 1964 would be 'The Four Modernizations.'[10] Mao ultimately took a different lesson. He blamed the peasants for being capitalist small producers under these post-Leap reforms and the Party for being corrupt and unable to undertake the Great Leap properly. He saw the resurgence of capitalism everywhere. In January 1962, even as he accepted nominal blame for the errors of the Leap, Mao prophetically declared: 'Never Forget Class Struggle!'

The Four Modernizations policy was the Party's response to the Great Leap's failures. It was a technocratic model based on a fundamental reliance on the saving graces of science and technology and *ordered* social life based on rational, consultative administration under a rectified Communist Party. The xenophobic reliance on the 'Chinese only' technology of the Leap, which had made a virtue of China's international isolation and increasing tensions with the USSR, was reversed as China sought international aid. Diplomatic recognition by France in 1964 was one result of this turn outward in the 1960s. In fact, the fundamental policies of reform China in the 1980s were on the table and under way by 1964, but they were soon suspended.

It was Mao who stopped the reform. The fundamental contradiction of the CCP has been the tension between the rational technocracy that is the Party and the charismatic authority of its supreme leader. Mao was the tragic hero for Deng Xiaoping and his colleagues – the leader who brought success to their revolution only to nearly kill it after taking power. Mao did not learn the same lessons from the tragedy of the Great Leap as his senior colleagues had. He saw traitors, saboteurs, and the return of capitalist oppression of the working people. While Mao was clearly both paranoid and ruthless, he was not wrong about the return of economic exploitation in the market-oriented reforms of the early 1960s under the CCP. Mao's solution was a return to active, violent revolution. His tool: *luan*, or chaos. And it worked, for a while. The chaos of student demonstrations, mutual denunciations among Party cadres, and orchestrated purges and public trials stopped the technocratic reforms dead and tossed the Party leadership that had led them out of office, into the streets and, ultimately, sent them down to the farm to starve or reform themselves according to the Great Leap goals of faith in Mao and Mao alone.

This was Mao's third and final great mass campaign, the Cultural Revolution.[11] In this he turned to youth, to students, to younger cadres to do what intellectuals and peasants had failed to do: rebel. In 1966 Mao famously declared, 'It is right to rebel!' He set factions within the CCP against each other, with his wife, Jiang Qing, leading the most leftist and most enthusiastically loyal to a charismatic reading of Mao's every utterance. With the 'little red book' (*Quotations of Chairman Mao Zedong*) they rode roughshod over the ruined careers and often the dead bodies of Mao's old revolutionary colleagues. Mao also set youth gangs onto the streets of China's cities and towns to 'crush the four olds,' to root out capitalist roaders, and to 'struggle against revisionists.' These were the famous Red Guards of the Cultural Revolution, the shock troops of Mao's rebellion against his own party. The social chaos, particularly in 1966 and 1967, racked China's cities and towns. In the name of Mao, in the name of the Revolution, Chinese tormented, abused, and killed each other. Mao brought the street violence to an end by calling in the People's Liberation Army to staff the decimated Party committees in institutions across China, and by sending the Red Guard student rebels to the countryside 'to learn from the masses.' By the time of Mao's death in 1976, the CCP was still picking up the pieces.

This is the contradictory legacy of Mao: while Mao wrote the norms and rules of CCP leadership and represents its successes, he is also the voice of rebellion and the mirror that shows up the faults and failures of the Party. The social results of this contradiction, and this history of Mao's three campaigns in the 1950s and 1960s, are profoundly important for China today. The most famous slogan of the tumultuous Cultural Revolution, 'it's right to rebel' (*zaofan youli*), trained a generation of Chinese youth. When those former Red Guards returned to urban China from their rustication after two, three, and sometimes ten years, they had learned from Mao, though not perhaps what Mao and the Party wanted them to learn. They learned of the profound corruptibility of the Party and of leaders everywhere, they learned it was possible – and that Mao agreed – to rebel against corrupt leadership, and they learned that rural China was still very poor. Not only poor, but also superstitious. Rural China has been identified with the excesses of faith in Mao that these self-same 'educated youth' also displayed during the 1960s and during at least some of their time in the countryside. The Beijing scholar Wang Yi has studied the links between Cultural Revolution Maoism and Chinese folk religion. Red Guards and many urban and rural Chinese had complete faith in Mao during much of the Cultural Revolution: '... Mao Zedong became the supreme and all-powerful super god, the "Sun that never sets."... They therefore paid homage to his image, sang Mao quotation songs, chanted his sayings, performed the Loyalty Dance (*zongzi wu*) and "struggled against self-interest and repudiated revisionism..." '[12] That intellectuals, in particular, indulged in these shamanistic rituals is not just a cause of great embarrassment today but the source of profound reflection – self-doubt for some, idealization of the West for others, cynicism and materialism for others, or virulent hatred of Mao or anyone else seen to be responsible for 'making me do it.'

Maoist orthodoxy: ideology in a secular age

The broadest result of this recent history, not only of the Cultural Revolution but of the victory of 1949 followed by the tribulations of the Hundred Flowers and Anti-Rightist Campaigns and the tragedy and waste of the Great Leap, has been the secularization of society. In Mao's time, as we have seen from the Loyalty Dances in the Cultural Revolution, Maoism was nearly a religion. It explained everything. Now there has been what Weber would have called a 'disenchantment,' a loss of blind faith, a secularization of politics. But this has not meant the end of ideology any more than ideology is absent from any other modern society. It does mean that the official orthodoxy of the CCP, Marxism-Leninism-Mao Zedong Thought, as well as doctrinal additions by Deng Xiaoping and even Jiang Zemin, no longer dominates people's minds across China, but the shared residual discourse of Maoism does shape their assumptions, expectations, and habitual ways of thinking.

Maoist orthodoxy is used by the CCP to provide the legitimacy that would otherwise come from the ballot box. The story of China's modern history that it tells is central to this legitimization and remains the one we saw Mao announce in 1940 in 'On New Democracy' (see above, p. 37). Whether or not various people in China believe every part of this official story, the basic assumptions about or identity of China that the CCP present are widely accepted. Thus, we need to distinguish between the specific and general claims made in Maoist orthodoxy. Today, most people in China do not claim to follow Mao's teachings, nor do they think the current Party is a noble example of Mao's or anyone's ideals. Yet most people in China appear to accept the assumptions in this story, about China's national identity, about the role of imperialism in China's history and present, and about the value of maintaining and improving this thing called China, and, increasingly, China's middle classes accept the additional story in Maoism: nationalism – China was great, was put down, and will rise again.

Politically, CCP orthodoxy now fulfills a function closer to political platforms among Western democratic political parties. It announces the policies, programs and goals of the Party and positions the Party to look good in the broader morality of public culture by claiming to do 'good things' for 'the good of the country.' Party orthodoxy particularly serves to announce the basic planks of policy. The most recent addition to the Maoist canon has been Jiang Zemin's theory of the 'Three Represents.' The 16th Party Congress held in Beijing in November 2002 enshrined Jiang's theory, even as he turned over the post of General Secretary – China's top political post – to his successor, Hu Jintao. Jiang's 'Three Represents' (*sangge daibiao*) says that the CCP 'should always represent the developmental requirements of China's advanced productive forces, represent the developing orientation of China's advanced culture, and represent the fundamental interests of the overwhelming majority of the Chinese people.'[13] While foreign observers and Chinese intellectuals alike scoff at these tortured formulations, they reflect the efforts of the still-ruling CCP to explain the massive changes of reform in terms that do not patently contradict Chinese Marxist-Leninist orthodoxy. If we utterly dismiss the slogans of the Party as 'political rubbish' or mere window-dressing, we will miss the actual policies of China's leaders and, more so, fail to understand how the CCP maintains its public legitimacy without democracy.

Jiang Zemin's Three Represents, indeed, point to very important changes in the CCP's leadership and policy goals. The 16th Party Congress included official Party representatives – that is, Party members – who are capitalists, or in current parlance private entrepreneurs. The phrase 'represent the [...] advanced productive forces' covers that change in Party membership. Similarly, 'interests of the overwhelming majority of the Chinese people' points to the official end of class struggle as a guiding policy of CCP rule. Finally, 'advanced culture' indicates the rewelcoming of intellectuals and the technical elite back into the CCP as it strives to garner public legitimacy as the party that can deliver social peace, economic growth, and cultural florescence. It also heralds a frank elitism that is not entirely alien to the Bolshevik party. As one commentator aptly notes, Jiang's formulation suggests 'that the Party will become a more elitist-oriented organization, with a new trinity of political (officials), economic (entrepreneurs and managers), and intellectual elites at its top level.'[14]

China's elite politics continues the shape, if not all of the content, of Mao period politics. In the absence of legitimization by elections, the 'core leader' of the Party, that is the General Secretary of the CCP, who is also made President of the PRC and chair of the Central Military Commission, is certified by a combination of factional politics and claims to 'great thought.' Thus, China's current 'core leader,' Hu Jintao, has to make or be seen to make his own theoretical contributions. He, and his premier, Wen Jiabao, have indeed set out to do so in ways that matter in concrete policy. If Jiang Zemin's 'Three Represents' theory pointed to the goals of *growth* and initiative by favoring the new entrepreneurial class and the cities of Newly Industrializing China (see Madsen's model of Three Chinas, Chapter 4, below), Hu Jintao's and Wen Jiabao's theoretical formulations address the burning issues of *equity*, social justice, and social order that have come to the fore as a result of a decade or more of single-minded, more or less neo-liberal developmentalism.

The new contender for admission to the Maoist canon is Hu Jintao's theory of 'Harmonious Society' (*hexie shehui*).[15] This spin on the Party platform focuses on the third of the Three Represents – the interests of the overwhelming majority of Chinese. It shifts the burning issues confronting the interior provinces, the downtrodden, and the losers of reform to front and center. The new emphasis on 'Harmonious Society,' however, will remind those familiar with Latin American history of other forms of authoritarian populism. On the one hand it draws attention to questions of social equity, but on the other hand it also signals intolerance of dissent or 'disturbances' by protestors. That such ideological policy platforms have political power can be seen by the impact of Hu and Wen's focus on equity at the recent 10th Session of the National People's Congress in Beijing in March 2006. The usually compliant legislature has balked on approving the government's draft law to protect property rights because that law is seen as serving the rich and disenfranchising the poor (particularly over the disposal of collective and state assets).[16]

The only other major public use of Maoism endorsed by the CCP is nationalism. The 1990s saw a strong swing to official nationalism with the CCP claiming loudly to be the national savior of China in the past and the only sure protector of national sovereignty and dignity today. This use of Maoism as a form of nationalism draws from a major part of Mao's writings, as we have seen, and it is broadly accepted by the public in China, but it is a two-edged sword. The CCP has spent as much time trying to quell popular nationalism and xenophobia in the past ten years, particularly against the USA and Japan, as it has trying to promote Chinese patriotism.[17] The problem with nationalism is its volatility. It is an effective tool for both the state and for members of the public. It works as one way to legitimize the rule of the CCP, but it also serves as the most obvious, useful, and frequently used form of legitimate public protest in China today. The state cannot be seen to oppose national dignity. Thus, protests against US affronts to China's national dignity (obligingly proffered by succeeding administrations in Washington) or against Japan's astonishing unwillingness to take seriously Chinese resentments from the Sino-Japanese War become a safe way for Chinese who are not happy with their lives today to hit the streets and protest. Nationalism in China can thus make the CCP and the government look very good or it can sanction public demonstrations that are very hard to control since they appear to be patriotic.

Beyond CCP use of Maoist orthodoxy, Mao's ideas exist in varying forms in the minds of ordinary Chinese. Maoism was directly studied by those who lived under Mao and in the early post-Mao years, less so by those schooled in the 1980s, and only in the most cursory fashion by younger generations (on the level of civics classes in Western school systems). Older generations feel a dismay at their

complicity in the excesses of Mao worship in the past. They pass that
caution on, directly or simply by ignoring ideology.

Maoist orthopraxy: continuing habits and expectations

Orthodox is what the state says; orthopraxy is what people do
with what the state hands them. Clearly there is often a huge gap
between the ideals and practices of a system – one need only think
of the United States or the Catholic Church, or for that matter our
local community. Yet there is a meaningful relationship between
orthodoxy and orthopraxy. In the name of state goals the government sets up or encourages social institutions and rewards some
behavior and punishes others. Whether or not a particular person
actually believes in the orthodoxy, if they wish to operate in the legal
society they must be seen to act in accordance with those stated
goals. In China under Mao this required loyalty to the Party line,
which generally extolled the virtues of the proletariat, the wickedness
of capitalists, and the salvationary role of the CCP and your local
Party leaders. More significantly for life in China today, this Maoist
orthodoxy also set up important *social institutions* that shaped life on
the ground. The three most important are the local Party committee
(at each and every level of government and in most large economic
and residential organizations), the *danwei* work unit organization of
employment, residence, and social insurance, and the *hukou* system
of internal residential passports. We met these social institutions
of the Mao period in Chapter 1. They have shaped social life even
as they have changed under the forces of market and international
contact during reform.

Participation without democracy The Party committee system embodied the CCP's claim that the legitimate forum for public policy
debate and policy formation was the Party itself, not the press, public
square, coffee house, classroom or proverbial kitchen debates. This
has produced a cautious reluctance to get involved in public affairs
because to do so is dangerous (think of the Anti-Rightist Campaign).
But the heritage of Maoism gives specific actors legitimate grounds,
and for those now in their forties and fifties actual social experience
in the Cultural Revolution, for organizing to resist oppression and

to seek redress from the Party. From the start of Maoism, some Party members used the orthodoxy to push the Party to do better. In 1942, a CCP translator and writer, Wang Shiwei, lampooned Mao in the newspapers of Yan'an and called on the CCP to live up to its ideals of egalitarianism and inner-party democracy. In the 1980s, even after the outrages of the Cultural Revolution, the president of the Science and Technology University and working astrophysicist Fang Lizhi used Party norms to argue for greater democratization. In between, brave individuals have stood up to local Party leaders to speak out against the abuses of power by using the norms and values embodied in Marxism-Leninism-Mao Zedong Thought.[18] This inclination to work within the Party-State system, and therefore to use – and creatively extend – the ideals and norms of the state orthodoxy, continues today. Wenfang Tang finds in his surveys of both establishment and non-establishment intellectuals today the belief that '[w]orking with the party elite is probably the most practical way to bring about concrete political improvement.'[19]

People in China continue to look to the *state* to solve public problems. This is an utterly sensible attitude in the face of consistent state repression of all alternative political and social movements since the 1940s. But it is a habit that shapes the assumptions of even democratic activists and frustrates the efforts of those who wish to organize citizen movements. The problem for both the Chinese state and Chinese citizens today is that the state is simply not big enough, nor does it have the institutional capacity, to do all that must be done across that vast continent and among the huge population that comprise China. A simple story captures this public reticence. An American academic working in Beijing in the late 1980s was struck by the mess in the hallway of his apartment building, which served a major research institution. The residents were all high-level intellectuals and professionals. Why not organize a simple residents' committee and hold a 'clean up day,' he suggested. His aghast Chinese colleagues replied that such matters were the domain of the authorities and to do what he suggested would be most presumptuous!

The divided heritage of Maoism in the practice of participation without democracy leaves people in China with the contradictory experiences of 'self-reliance' (*zili gengsheng*) and even models of more or less forthright criticism of the CCP and also examples of the passivity and going-along that got most people through the Cultural Revolution. These contrasting models of behavior lie in the 'toolbox' of Chinese seeking to make their way in the more socially isolated environment of market socialism.

Eating from the big family pot Daily life in the work units and communes reinforced this political passivity and dependency. The state work unit system, or *danwei*, under Mao created a collective economy at the basic level in which everything but small personal effects was owned by the group. These *danwei* became a veritable work-related clan defined by permanent employees and their families. They shouldered the responsibility of providing not only employment but housing, education, medical care, and other daily life necessities for their members. Elizabeth Perry summarizes the attributes of this ubiquitous organization of work and life in urban China under Mao. The *danwei* had power over personnel matters (hiring, firing, maintaining dossiers), it provided communal facilities for housing, dining, health, etc. (often in the form of a walled compound), it maintained independent accounts and budgets, it was urban and not rural, and it was public, part of the state system.[20] This work unit system created a mutual dependency in which the individual gave up a great deal of individual choice in exchange for very high expectations that the group would take care of each individual. Ironically, farmers in the collectivized organization of the communes were not cared for nearly as much – they had neither social insurance nor pensions, for example. But they shared the norms of collective ownership and group decision-making with their compatriots in the urban *danwei*.

This enforced passivity – from political experience and workplace organization – is a major hurdle. Reformers in the state and party apparatus are actively seeking ways to mobilize various groups in China to get the work of governance and economic activity done. Yet these reformers are constrained by the one-party state orthodoxy. They have the nearly impossible task of energizing people to act in the public arena but not to challenge the Party's monopoly of political power.

Habits of thought Those who lived through the Maoist system carry with them the habits of thought and expectations that made sense under Mao's rule. This population, long corralled by the rules of non-democratic participation in *danwei* and commune life, does not have the habits of mind suitable to a liberal or tolerant society. These same habits and expectations even shape those who reject official Maoism and embrace alternative political ideas and social practices. Inevitably, some part of these values and expectations has been passed on – by parents and teachers – to younger genera- tions. Naturally, they change with time and new experiences, but these mental models still shape the experiences and reactions of people in China. Central among these hegemonic values are respect for intellectuals, intolerant modes of argument and illiberal public demonstrations, and the expectation that suggestions should be addressed to the state. It is this mental furniture that will shape the lives of people in China long after the *hukou* passports and *danwei* work units are a thing of the past.

INTELLECTUALS in China are the envy of Western China scholars. In China, intellectuals are taken seriously both by the state and the public. That is one reason why the CCP has always bothered to repress unorthodox intellectuals – because the Party believes that what intellectuals say is influential. While this is changing, and intellectuals in reform China constantly bemoan their recent mar- ginalization, nonetheless a residual respect for certified intellectuals remains in Chinese society that distinguishes it from all others. As we saw in the Preface, it was this residual respect for intellectuals and students which contributed mightily to popular support for student demonstrations in Tiananmen in 1989. This deference to intellectuals continues today both in the expectation that highly educated professionals and cultural commentators in China ought to help figure out what to do, and in cynicism and criticism of them for failure to do so in most cases. Respect for intellectuals has been transformed under global capital in the reform period to a broad reliance on *experts* to advise the Party and business. There is not, as yet, a widespread acceptance that good governance can come from the democracy of 'one man, one vote' in China.

MORAL EXTREMISM characterizes public debate on hot issues in China. China is not without intelligent and rational, indeed brilliant, scholars, theorists, and political reformers, but the nature of public debate has, in practice, all too quickly reverted to the moral extremism of Maoism when the going gets tough. Westerners who follow China's relations with the USA or Japan know how quickly diplomatic issues – from the Belgrade bombing of the Chinese embassy by NATO forces in 1999 to the revival of the history textbook issue with Japan in 2005 – go to rhetorical extremes. This is not the result of propaganda manipulation by the CCP; it comes from deep in the belly of ordinary Chinese. As Suisheng Zhao has shown, this popular nationalism bedevils efforts by the CCP to promote a more predictable state nationalism or attempts by some intellectuals to advocate a liberal nationalism that addresses, as well, domestic issues of social justice.[21]

Geremie Barmé notes the continuity of this intolerant language – even among the official supporters of reform and opening. He gives the example of a 1992 book that is critical of old-style leftism in the Party. The preface praises Deng Xiaoping's famous 'Southern Tour' (see Chapter 3, below) of 1992 which supported continued reform, but the preface's style reflects the continued force of Maoist moral extremism even as it criticizes 'left' resistance to Deng's economic reforms:

> At the crucial moment when the powers of extreme 'leftism' and their in-house theoreticians, swollen with arrogance, had set their sights on striking out wantonly against reform, Comrade Deng Xiaoping resolutely toured the south. He issued speeches in which he stated categorically: 'We must guard against rightism, but more important, we must prevent "leftism"!' One simple sentence, but each word bears the weight of greatness ... Oh, how fortunate the reforms! How blessed are our people![22]

A vivid example of these residual habits of intolerance came in 2005 from a former Red Guard and notable author in English, Jung Chang. Her recent biography of Mao is a stunning piece of Maoist anti-Maoism, attacking Mao in very much the manner of the extreme, one-sided, and hyperbolic campaigns she participated in herself in the Cultural Revolution.[23] Jung Chang portrays Mao as an evil, power- and sex-hungry sadist who worked for his personal advantage in the most despicable ways, relying on trickery, manipulation, and terror. Mao *never* did anything for the good of anyone else; *none* of his policies *ever* worked. He was bad, bad, bad. In fact, he was the ultimate counter-revolutionary! This is the most ironic legacy of Maoism – even a former Red Guard living in London who wants to purge herself of her former adulation of Mao feels compelled to use the very methods of 'mass criticism' which Mao perfected under his rule to attack Mao's memory today. While the results are unconvincing for most readers in English, the moral extremism, the black-and-white judgments, resonate with many readers in China. Thus, one does not have to be a Maoist, or in this case to like anything Mao did, in order to carry on Maoist habits of thought and argument.

Jung Chang exhibits the fury of the apostate, but she is not alone in her moral extremism. Even China's most elite academic intellectuals – working in the major universities of Beijing and Shanghai – cannot seem to resist such 'spit fights.' In the late 1990s this was characterized by an acrimonious debate between those who supported liberalism, more or less along the lines of neo-liberal policies associated with von Hayek, and those who borrowed postmodern critiques from the West to recast a left attack on capital. The fight between liberals and the New Left amused but disheartened observers, such as Shanghai public intellectual Xu Jilin, who nearly despaired of finding a way to get various intellectual factions to work together instead of attacking each other. The fights have continued, leading Xu, among others, to bemoan the balkanization of Chinese intellectual life (see Chapter 4, below). The role of the Internet has, alas, been pernicious, enabling libelous exchanges and outrageous claims and counter-claims to find a ready audience. In 2000 money added fuel to the fire. Li Kai-shing, the Hong Kong-based billionaire, gave some HK$60 million to the Chinese Ministry of Education to support research. Part of that money went to a 'Cheung Kong-*Reading* Award' for the best articles in the journal *Reading* (*Dushu*). A huge Internet brawl broke out when it was discovered that one of the winners was Wang Hui, one of the editors of *Reading.* The level of vitriol and polemical rhetoric is what stands out in this 'intellectual exchange.'[24]

TALK TO THE PARTY The upshot, as Wenfang Tang's survey research has confirmed, is that when intellectuals or social activisits are not fighting each other, they are talking to the Party-State. This is born of both habit and of pragmatism. As we have seen, the CCP will not tolerate a substantial social organization or movement outside its control, from Christian house churches to Falungong to any sort of political party. Working people assume it is up to the 'leaders,' or at least to the certified intellectuals, to fix things. Intellectuals cast their suggestions in terms of, or at least carefully not in contradiction to, Party ideological platforms, and most work for the state in one fashion or another – in universities, academies of science or social science, or major industries. This state orientation of civil society has been a real challenge to Western observers, who persist in seeing sprouts of individual democratic activity. It may come, but so far lived experience, intellectual orientation, and even business practices (in which business actors survive by colluding with local political leaders in the absence of legal protections) all point to collaboration with the Party-State rather than confrontation.

To focus on working with the Party does not imply absolute passivity. There were some 86,000 violent 'incidents' (demonstrations, attacks on enterprise or local leaders, even riots) in 2005. Rural Chinese have suffered the most, and they have acted the most, as we shall see in later chapters. But the point to keep in mind is: they are not organizing. No peasants' union, no local or national political party, no cross-district associations – despite the technical capabilities of cell phones and the Internet. Each demonstration – even when violent – is specific in issue (back pay, compensation for land taken, redress for official abuse or the effects of pollution) and focused on local leaders. We are seeing only the beginnings of what the CCP feared in Tiananmen – intellectuals linking with working people. When a Beijing-based lawyer traveled to a small town in Guangdong to represent local farmers who had been beaten by police during a demonstration in 2004, he, in turn, was detained, beaten, and driven away. Independent advocacy, so far, has not produced much in China. Hence the continuing conversations with the Party-State.

Living Maoism is the software that runs on the hardware of China's physical and human geography. These two systems come from history but are active and reproduced in daily life. Of course they change – population increases, people move, a housing market was created, new ideas are incorporated – but the changes are incremental. The inherited institutions and patterns plus these developments of them are the social realities from which the post-Mao reforms sprang and through which they continue to operate. With the immense diversity yet shared identity of the peoples across China in mind, and with the living social and mental legacies of Maoism before us we can better make sense of why the CCP initiated renewed reforms in the late 1970s and how the ongoing interaction between political intent and social experience has shaped living with reform.

3 | Reform: Mao is dead, long live Mao!

Reform defines China today. Where did it come from? When did it start? What were its goals and have those goals changed over time? How did it work, especially across China's vast systems of different communities? Did this reform contradict Maoism? The great irony of the post-Mao reforms, which most people date from the late 1970s, is that in many ways they are a continuation of reforms that began under Mao, and they have been carried out by a Maoist leadership, the CCP. Mao Zedong did not promote a capitalist market, private property and foreign investment, but he did set a pattern of bold (and sometimes reckless) policy experimentation. Deng Xiaoping, the architect and leader of China's contemporary reforms from 1974 until his death in 1997, was in many ways the last Maoist, even as he used Mao's political style and leadership skills to reverse the concrete policies of Mao's later years.

This chapter reviews in brief compass the intentions of China's current reform from its beginning in the 1970s. It came from the top, the Leninist elite, and not from the intellectuals or public, yet at least in the realm of rural decollectivization the CCP leadership had the sense to popularize what farmers in Anhui province had started to do on their own. The major steps of actual reform take us from the purge of the Leftists (who received the politically posthumous title of 'The Gang of Four') in 1976 to the seminal CCP resolution on Party history of 1981, which apportioned blame for the Cultural Revolution, through the halting and contradictory reform efforts of the 1980s, to the build-up and explosion of the great crisis of reform of 1989 at Tiananmen, followed by retrenchment and, finally, the successful synthesis made by Deng Xiaoping in 1992 in his famous 'Southern Tour': economic openness and reform without political liberalization. That policy still rules today.

The history of the creation and first twenty years of reform, from the 1970s to the early 1990s, demonstrates three fundamental points about China's politics and economy that are crucial for understanding China today:

1. Political and economic reform took off from Mao's death in 1976, but this did not entail a wholesale rejection of his thinking, his legacy, or previous Party experiments in governance. The year 1978 is a reasonable date to mark the start of the current 'reform and opening' under Deng Xiaoping and the rejection of radical socialism and international isolation during the previous Cultural Revolution. These reform policies, however, built on specific policies of the 'Four Modernizations' put forward by the Party in 1964 and make use of a tradition of bold experimentation in the CCP dating back to their earliest rural 'base areas' in the 1920s. This incomplete de-Maoification complicated efforts to steer reform through the 1980s and contributed to the crisis of 1989. It continues to bedevil Chinese politics today as the dispossessed legitimately quote Mao's populist writings to criticize the government.

2. Chinese politics has been animated by one specific legacy of the Cultural Revolution – the notion that mass participation can easily lead to chaos (or *luan*, 乱). Indeed, democracy itself is seen by many, inside and outside the government, as a form of *luan*. Party and public anxieties about social disorder help explain the machinations of CCP policy in the years leading up to 1989 and Tiananmen. These anxieties continue to animate Chinese politics today as China's current leaders continue to avoid democratization at almost any cost.

3. Deng Xiaoping chose not to replace Mao directly and rule as a charismatic leader (in the way, say Kim Jong-Il has succeeded to Kim Il-Song in North Korea). Rather, Deng chose to strengthen the role of the Party organization and to establish a more rigid and consistent bureaucratic base for CCP rule in China. Deng managed to slay the dragon of Stalinist dictatorship, but his bloodless coup came at the expense of enshrining cronyism and corruption in the political process.

Not the Cultural Revolution: the beginnings of reform

Chairman Mao died on 9 September 1976. His departure set in motion forces for change that had been building for several years. First, the radical leadership around Mao was removed that October and denounced as 'The Gang of Four.' Next, a compromise leadership was confirmed under the obscure Party functionary Hua Guofeng, who declared a 'victorious conclusion' to the Cultural Revolution in 1977. Then the Party announced a renewed modernization program that emphasized science, technology, and calm, rational management. This was a revival of the Four Modernizations policy from 1964 that had been sidelined by the Cultural Revolution. Finally, internal Party squabbles on how China should reform were settled in a now famous Party plenum in December 1978 which saw the return to power of Deng Xiaoping. Reform China was on its way.

These beginnings of reform in China were cast in terms of the Cultural Revolution, Mao's tumultuous last revolution. As we saw in Chapter 2, the massive political campaign began with student demonstrations and intellectual purges in 1966 and led to nearly a decade of upheaval, political purges, and social repression. The Cultural Revolution showed the fatal flaws of Maoism. When the charismatic leader demanded unreasonable and, indeed, immoral acts, the CCP turned out to be unable to stop the chaos. For the CCP that fears social chaos, the irony is, of course, that the chaos of the Cultural Revolution was instigated at the top, by their own leader, Mao Zedong. The key figure for China of the lessons of the Cultural Revolution is Deng Xiaoping himself. A veteran of the famous Long March of the CCP in 1934–35, and already a top Party leader in the 1950s, Deng was purged in the Cultural Revolution but survived (ironically owing to Mao's intercession). Deng was returned to power in 1974 by Mao to bring the state administration back into order. The radical faction (later 'The Gang of Four') engineered Deng's second purge in spring 1976, however.

After his return to real leadership in late 1978, Deng Xiaoping led the CCP, which was still internally divided among at least radicals, moderates, and technocrats, with one guiding thought: to reverse the mistakes of the Cultural Revolution under which nearly all of them, and so many of the people in China, had suffered. Thus, the effective leadership coalition of reform China in the 1980s cohered more around the negative goal of undoing the Cultural Revolution. Chaos (*luan*) is the single most common descriptor of the Cultural Revolution and the avoidance of *luan* has been a key part of CCP ideology over the past twenty-five years. Modernization, openness to the West, relaxing the strict social controls of *hukou* internal passports or *danwei* work unit rules are all predicated on this primary goal because Party leaders have hoped that these reforms will contribute to economic development and thus to calming the restless claims of a public that is not satisfied with poverty-line existence and repressive politics. Observers of reform China have wondered at the apparent contradiction between the economic flexibility and openness of the CCP and its political inflexibility and authoritarianism. It is the history of the Cultural Revolution and the person of Deng Xiaoping which help explain why this is not a contradiction to China's leadership. Both economic reform and political control contribute to the shared overriding goal of stability and to the avoidance of *luan*.

The first step in preventing a return of the *luan* of the Cultural Revolution for Deng Xiaoping was to guarantee that there could never again be a supreme leader like Mao who could unleash chaos on the Party. The CCP loves history, and twice in its career the Party has issued 'Historical Resolutions' to confirm the legitimacy of a major new orientation in policy. The first was in 1945, at the 7th Party Congress, to confirm Mao Zedong as Party Chairman and Helmsman of the Chinese Revolution. The second was in 1981, under the de facto rule of Deng Xiaoping, to put Mao squarely into history and China firmly on the track to economic reform and international engagement. The goals of the reform leadership were announced in the 'Resolution on Certain Questions in the History of our Party since the Founding of the People's Republic of China,' which was passed at the Sixth Plenum of the Eleventh CCP Central Committee on 27 June 1981.[1] Its main purpose was to lay the Cultural Revolution to rest and to account for Mao's failings without undermining his role as the legitimization of the CCP. The resolution lay down a narrative, a way to think about China's revolutionary history more or less since Mao's own characterization of the Party's leadership in 1940 in 'On New Democracy' (discussed in Chapter 2, above). Thus, the 1981 Historical Resolution begins with a litany of achievements of Party rule up to 1966 – passing lightly over the disasters of the Great Leap. 'All the successes in these ten years were achieved under the collective leadership of the Central Committee of the Party headed by Comrade Mao Zedong. Likewise, responsibility for the errors committed in the work of this period rested with the same collective leadership.'

Indeed, collective leadership and Party organization are the theme of the Historical Resolution – claiming the organizational side of Maoism and laying aside the charismatic parts. But collective leadership and an organizational approach do not, as many Westerners might think, spell the end of ideology. This key document for reform China is all about ideology; the issue was simply *which* sort of ideology the CCP should follow. 'Many outstanding leaders of our Party made important contributions to the formation and development of Mao Zedong Thought,' the Historical Resolution declares, 'and they are synthesized in the scientific works of Comrade Mao Zedong ... ' The collective nature of this body of political wisdom is emphasized in order to justify not only the relevance of Mao Zedong Thought but also to *certify the surviving leaders*: they were contributors to this ideology and thus are the legitimate leaders of China. 'Mao Zedong Thought is the valuable spiritual asset of our Party. It will be our guide to action for a long time to come. The Party leaders and the large group of cadres nurtured by Marxism-Leninism and Mao Zedong Thought were the backbone forces in winning great victories for our cause; they are and will remain our treasured mainstay in the cause of Socialist modernization.' The prophet is gone, but the Church remains.

The Cultural Revolution remains the dominant explanatory variable (or excuse) for everything that has happened in China in the 1970s and 1980s. It continues to define (usually by negative contrast) Chinese understandings of what they are trying to achieve through 'reform.' This is an approach shared by Chinese leaders, many around China, and even most Western academics, but the emphasis on the impact of the Cultural Revolution obscures the continuities in ideology and social practices from the entire Mao period (including the 1950s) that continue to shape life in China today.[2] In Chapter 2 we saw some of these living legacies of Maoism in participation without democracy, depending on intellectuals or leaders to organize solutions, and an intolerant tone in public debates. At the same time, the goals of social equity from Mao's broader corpus of writings, as well as from the Cultural Revolution, still resonate with many in the CCP and across China. Since Deng Xiaoping and the reform leadership have chosen not to repudiate Mao's heritage even as they reverse most of his policies – as they neither want to abandon their revolutionary heritage nor can afford to forgo the legitimization of Mao's mantle – they face the constant danger that some starving farmer, unemployed worker, or displaced resident will find embarrassing statements from Maoist thought, which the Party still recognizes as a 'valuable spiritual asset' and a 'guide to action.'

Reform and openness in the 1980s and the road to Tiananmen

As we saw in Chapter 2, China's current economic reforms began after the failures of the Great Leap in the early 1960s, but were cut short by the Cultural Revolution. Thus, when Deng Xiaoping returned to power – first in 1974 and most securely in 1978 – he went straight back to the 1964 reforms but with the added urgency of avoiding the threat of charismatic leadership. He addressed the second problem in two ways. First, he refused to take up Mao's mantle as 'Chairman.' The august position of *zhuxi* or Chairman was by the end of the Cultural Revolution inseparably linked to Mao's charisma and to the chiliastic excesses of both that campaign and the earlier Great Leap. Since Deng Xiaoping was in fact the supreme leader with widely acknowledged revolutionary credentials among his colleagues, he could and did use his revolutionary charisma to blunt the public charisma of the Party Chairman. He did this by ensuring that the post of Chairman would lapse with the uncharismatic Hua Guofeng, who was eclipsed from real power by Deng and his associates by 1980. This required the Party apparatus to return to its earlier Leninist norms of committee work under the General Secretary of the Central Committee of the CCP, now the highest post in China. The first new General

Secretary was Hu Yaobang, appointed at the same 12th Congress of the CCP in 1982 that abolished the position of Chairman. While the CCP is not a democratic party, it is an organized one with a bureaucratic hierarchy and lines of authority. Deng Xiaoping's first and fundamental act was to restore Leninist administrative order. This has produced the coherent and stable government that has overseen China's reforms for a quarter-century, but it has institutionalized the corruption of an unelected Party that cannot control the excesses of its local officials.[3] This last problem is an unpaid bill confronting China today.

Deng Xiaoping's second attack on charismatic leadership has been a careful de-Maoification, as we have seen in his 1981 Historical Resolution, above. The trick has been to sap the awe of Mao in both the public mind and among rank-and-file Party cadres while not killing the revolutionary goose that has laid the golden egg. Mao is the touchstone for CCP political legitimacy as an unelected party. To discredit Mao utterly would be to make the mistake of Khrushchev, who undermined the CPSU in his accurate denunciations of Stalin. Deng Xiaoping's solution was his famous assessment of Mao as '70% correct and 30% incorrect,' that is, imperfect (and thus subject to revision based on practice) but still mostly good (and thus still a source of legitimacy for the Party). This was enshrined politically in the Central Committee's 1981 Historical Resolution. For Deng and his colleagues, this laid the Cultural Revolution to rest and freed them to pursue the Four Modernizations without distraction. This compromise solution has, however, complicated Party efforts to put economic and political reform into practice, since Mao's writings include numerous statements against capitalist restoration!

Reform as experimentation Deng Xiaoping's reforms did not go smoothly. In addition to the internal contradictions between social and economic relaxation while maintaining political authoritarianism, the Four Modernizations program was bedeviled by residual political resistance among the leadership and rank and file, who either felt the de facto capitalist nature of the reforms was a repudiation of socialism and Mao's ideals or, regardless of ideological niceties, saw their privileges threatened. These people coalesced around the senior figure, Chen Yun, the only Party leader of rank, experience, and prestige to challenge Deng Xiaoping – even though the two leaders were not necessarily competitors politically. Throughout the 1980s these two 'political parties' within the CCP contested. Deng Xiaoping, however, was a wily politician, second only to Mao in his ability to manipulate the Chinese political system. He did not become the leader of the reform group within the Party. He engineered the appointment of a young reformist leader and his protégé, Hu Yaobang, as General Secretary in 1982. This left Deng as the kingmaker and arbiter as the forces around the party reformers and party traditionalists debated goals, put forward policies, and tried to subvert each other's programs. After many ups and downs, social changes in China gave market-oriented reforms the edge and, despite the turmoil of Tiananmen and the temporary return of the traditional party model in 1990, Deng's reform model prevailed and the advocates of state planning and limited contact with global capital and media lost influence.

From the start, the reforms in China have been characterized by two things. First, *experimentation*, the open-ended, indeed, unclear path. Only the general goal has been shared by the various leadership factions in the CCP – wealth and power for China and never again the chaos of the Cultural Revolution. Second, given the lack of consensus at the top on *how* to make China strong and prosperous, at each step along the way the *reactions* to reform from people and groups across China have helped shape government policy. Sometimes it has been the spontaneous action of farmers, as in the initial decollectivization in the early 1980s, sometimes the actions of local officials who went on a construction spending spree in the 1980s and overheated the economy, and sometimes it has been the collective protests of those unhappy with the injustices of reform, as we have seen in the student demonstrations in Tiananmen in 1989, and which continue in villages and neighborhoods across China as displaced workers or residents of polluted communities take their grievances to the government or to the streets.

The story of reform in the 1980s is one of experimentation leading to unanticipated results, and so to leadership squabbles that produced swings in policy to speed up or slow down the changes.

In the end, by 1989 the leadership was in a deadlock and the urban public, in particular, was fed up. Despite astonishing changes – as a China that had been 'closed' to the West for thirty years really did open up, life on the ground became more relaxed, open, and colorful, and the economy really did expand impressively – by 1989 there were real and pressing problems. Two issues brought people, especially urban residents, to the street: the worst inflation in PRC history and the perception that official corruption was now worse than at any time since 1949. We will look at the experience of reform for various people across China in the next chapter. Here we want to get a sense of how the first decade and a half of reform and opening (1978–92) looked to China's leaders, including how they responded to the challenges of unintended consequences along the way.[4] We focus on the Party leadership because they have been the ones with the power to initiate and put limits on reform.

The CCP's initial reform policies were announced at the Third Plenum of the Eleventh Central Committee in December 1978. As we saw in Chapter 1, the Party and its top institutions – the Party Congress, the plenums of its Central Committee, its politburo and standing Committee – set government policy in China. The Third Plenum set Deng Xiaoping's reform goals. First, it made economic modernization the central goal of Party work. Second, it began to address the wounds of the Cultural Revolution by reversing verdicts on Party cadres who had been purged by Mao (this would culminate in the 1981 Historical Resolution, discussed above). Third, the plenum approved experimentation with market forces, beginning the breaking open of the planned economy. The slogan from that time was 'practice' – and it would produce the key slogan of the 1980s, 'practice is the sole criterion of truth.' These policies were implemented over the next few years in a series of administrative changes designed to 'open' China to the world and to the market and to extricate the CCP from daily management of farming, factories, and business.

The heart of this first wave of reforms was decollectivization, in which the communes established in the late 1950s were broken up. Land was not returned to the individual farmer, but to the natural village which, in turn, leased individual family farming plots for at first fifteen years (now that has been extended to fifty years). In the cities, reform in the state owned enterprises (SOEs) was much slower, but management authority was given to enterprise managers, along with some freedom to keep profits above the State Plan and some responsibility to cover their unit's own debts. Party leaders could not agree on whether to adjust the centrally planned economy or give over to a market system. Piecemeal policies pushed first for more enterprise reform and then retrenched to more central planning. There was considerable confusion.

In addition to rural and industrial reform, the Party began to experiment with administrative reform. In the countryside, it replaced the administrative role of the 55,000 People's Communes with 96,000 rural townships, making this lowest level of formal administration more effective by having to care for a smaller population each. Administrative reform also included the promise of more citizenship participation, of some more democracy. But what this meant was not entirely clear at first. For example, there were local elections in municipal districts within Beijing in the early 1980s, but the Party got nervous and reverted to administrative appointment of local leaders.

Reaction and adjustment: Democracy Wall and intellectual debate The issue of democracy became one of the first challenges to the leadership arising from the unanticipated consequences of reform. Mao Zedong, after all, had declared the Cultural Revolution to be a form of 'big democracy' for the revolutionary masses. In the 1980s, the challenges to Party policies started at the top, among China's prestigious intellectuals inside the Party and its major universities. Hot debates on the reform of socialism, advocating socialist humanism and Party reform, as well as exposing in detail the errors of the Great Leap and Cultural Revolution, scandalized the political public in China's cities. The party traditionalists feared that too much criticism would bring *luan*. The result was a political seesaw of thaw and repression.

In 1978 Democracy Wall in Beijing caught worldwide attention. Could China be going democratic already? For some heady weeks in December 1978 Beijing residents could stroll down to the Xidan district and read astonishing posters that talked about the (until recently) unmentionable: the abuses of the Cultural Revolution. These were the same 'big character posters' that Red Guards had used in the Cultural Revolution to denounce 'capitalist roaders' and 'Soviet revisionists' inside the Party, but now this form of Maoist democracy was turned on the abuses and suffering of the Cultural Revolution and pointedly called upon the CCP to make amends. 'Democracy,' declared a wall-poster by an electrician at the Beijing Zoo, Wei Jingsheng, 'is the *fifth* modernization!' China seemed, in the words of one international journalist, to be 'coming alive.'

During his visit to the USA in 1978 to secure recognition of China by the world's dominant economy and power, Deng Xiaoping let the press wonder about Democracy Wall. Domestically, the revelations of abuses of power by the radical leadership also served to discredit remaining leaders in the CCP who were closely associated with the Cultural Revolution and who were standing in the way of Deng's reforms. America recognized China at the end of 1978. In spring 1979, Democracy Wall was unceremoniously moved to a small park in western Beijing, and those who wished to put up posters had to register their name and address with the authorities. By fall the leaders of Democracy Wall (most notably Wei Jingsheng) had been arrested, tried, and jailed. Public advocacy of political democracy of the liberal or parliamentary sort came to an end then, as the Four Basic Principles by Deng Xiaoping in March 1979 (which insisted that all public acts should uphold socialism and support Party leadership) became the new law.[5] It became clear from this example that Deng Xiaoping's tolerance of political free speech was tactical rather than substantive. It also became clear that the Party could and would shut down inconvenient public speech or assembly by force.

Intellectual agitation for change moved to the safer channels of the Party press, think tanks, and universities. These establishment channels frightened the Party much less. Indeed, various leaders hurried to gather together their own think tanks and professors to 'research' their policy preferences. In the early 1980s reform intellectuals backed by one or other Party leader pushed for a latitudinarian interpretation of Maoism that focused on the need to protect individual and collective rights against the abuses of those in power.[6] The language was that of the young Marx and the Marxist conception of alienation. Beyond the intricacies of Marxist theory (rendered into Chinese philosophical vocabulary), the bottom line of advocates of Marxist humanism was to push for some form of accountability and to strengthen the norms of inner-Party democracy. Wang Ruoshui, an editor at the *People's Daily*, raised the issue of 'alienation' under socialism and the need for the Party to focus on individuals and not disembodied social classes. The debate over alienation and Marxist humanism raged in the official press in 1983 and 1984. Some even dared suggest popular elections, at least at the grass-roots level. This brought on official repression in a warmed-over political campaign, the Campaign Against Spiritual Pollution, in 1984, and again in 1987, as the 'Anti-Bourgeois Liberalization' campaign. These were more than the purge of irritating or inconvenient intellectuals. These theorists were not dissidents, they were both Party members and in positions of influence. Many were employed, supported, and protected by Deng Xiaoping's General Secretary, Hu Yaobang, and, to a lesser degree, by the head of the state administration, Premier Zhao Ziyang. These debates were the public face of inner-Party divisions over the nature and directions of reform: was the State Plan to remain? Were markets to take over? What would be the role of the CCP? Of Maoism?

These debates were also national in character. The public sphere of Maoist China had been a 'directed public sphere' of the CCP's propaganda department. The press, radio, and very soon TV were centrally controlled and heavily censored. The major newspapers were limited – the *People's Daily*, the *Guangming Daily*, and *Liberation Daily* – but they were available more or less for free everywhere. As the central leadership experimented and argued over reform, these tools of propaganda became avenues for public discussion that was much livelier and varied than had been the case under Mao. In short, if an intellectual or policy advisor, such as Wang Ruoshui, could get an article on Marxist alienation into the *People's Daily* (as he did), then not only intellectuals and professionals across China could read it, but also workers and farmers and cadres in the villages. This was not a free public sphere, but it was a coherent national public sphere. While the proposals and suggestions that survived the censor's pen were incremental rather than revolutionary, they reached the broadest possible audience and built a public presumption that reform was good, necessary, and needed to be open to taking chances. The increased press freedom of the late 1990s, we shall see in later chapters, has come at the cost of a balkanization of the public sphere in China – there is no media outlet that is truly national. China's diverse communities are increasingly free to ignore each other.

Meanwhile, by 1985 the economy was in trouble. The flurry of economic energy released by rural decollectivization had slowed by 1984, and the government's abolition of mandatory grain purchases in 1985 depressed agricultural prices. Farmers began to be squeezed by the classic scissors effect – rising costs for inputs (fertilizer and pesticides) and falling prices for produce. Farmers began to look to sideline industries for more cash, to move away from grain to specialized crops, and to migration to the towns and cities for urban employment. Importantly, farmers experienced these changes as a promise broken and they complained. In the cities, the transition to a more market-oriented economy was painful, as well. The incentive system for enterprises, involving relaxation of the State Plan and price controls, led to overheating of the economy and a surge in inflation by 1985. The response of the CCP leadership, under Premier Zhao Ziyang, was put forth in April 1986 as the Seventh Five-Year Plan. Barry Naughton rates it as 'one of the most realistic and sound plans ever promulgated in China.'[7] Zhao proposed further extension of market mechanisms, in essence a gradual 'growing out of the plan,' under the slogan 'socialist commodity market.'

Resistance to reform – from inside the Party Politics intervened, however. The trouble wasn't on the streets or in the salons, it was in the halls of power and stemmed from the incomplete de-Maoification of Deng Xiaoping's reforms. There were strong forces inside the CCP and the military that were not happy with such reform plans. Three major groups opposed reform. First, the leaders and officials who ran the planned economy. They found their advocate in the senior leader Chen Yun. He supported a role for the market, but only in support of the Plan. This group worried about lower grain production, the growing gap between the developing coastal regions and the interior provinces, and the explosion of corruption which they saw as a result of more liberalized policies and contact with the West. To this group, reform was leading to *luan*. Second, orthodox Party leaders such as Peng Zhen worried about the social consequences of reform for the social fabric of China. This group took seriously the moral claims of Maoism and saw in the vibrant but uncontrolled changes of the early 1980s the 'corrosive influence of decadent bourgeois ideology and remnant feudal ideas.' While no supporters of radical Maoism, these members of the Party's ideological organizations still believed in 'socialist spiritual civilization' and saw the need for the Party to educate the public and protect the weak from the ravages of bourgeois markets. Of course, they felt that they themselves were best suited to undertake this task as teachers of society.[8] Third, senior military leaders also held to a similar socially conservative version of Maoism. They didn't like the 'disorder' of the newly freed social life and even less did they like recent cuts in their budgets.[9]

Resistance inside the Party to reform coalesced around a leadership fight against Deng's current successor, General Secretary Hu Yaobang. Demonstrations by students in December 1986, which Hu failed to suppress with sufficient vigor, frightened the Party elite and provided the opportunity to dismiss Hu Yaobang in January 1987 and to slow down reform. This success for the Party traditionalists also saw the public 'Anti-Bourgeois Liberalization' campaign that, among other things, expelled reformist editor Wang Ruoshui. This 1987 retrenchment against market and political reform succeeded in having Hu Yaobang criticized and purged. In contrast to the practice of earlier years, however, Hu was not demonized, humiliated, and imprisoned (or killed). In fact, he maintained his Party membership and comfortable living situation, but he was politically neutralized. In his stead, Deng Xiaoping moved the premier, Zhao Ziyang, to become the new Party leader (General Secretary). The tensions between party traditionalists and party reformers did not lessen; they increased. While Zhao Ziyang was a reformer, his successor as premier (at the top of the NPC and state government structure) was a Party conservative, Li Peng. Deng Xiaoping was performing his balancing act.

Yet reform was not to be stopped. As far as political leadership was concerned, this was because Deng Xiaoping remained committed to the basic line of reform: no charismatic rubbish, market liberalization, opening to the world, *and* continued Party rule. Thus, the 13th Party Congress in October 1987 recommitted to reform under the slogan 'initial stage of socialism.' This odd slogan explained the market – indeed, capitalist – reforms of the CCP in terms of orthodox Marxist-Leninist theory – China had to pass through actual and developed capitalist modes of production before 'fully' coming to socialism. This way of looking at reform policy may seem tortured to outsiders, but it made sense to insiders, as it allowed both economic and administrative reform while maintaining the commitment to the Party's ordering of society.

The compromise did not hold, mostly because the social consequences of reform sharpened. On the one hand, Party traditionalists were increasingly worried that the Party was losing control of changes in society. Ideology and what intellectuals wrote mattered to leaders such as Peng Zhen and Propaganda Department director Deng Lichun. And they did not like what they saw. In particular, the president of China's prestigious Science and Technology University in Hefei, Anhui, Dr Fang Lizhi, made a trenchant critique of CCP science policy and, more unforgivably, a cogent rebuttal of the scientistic assumptions of Frederick Engels. 'Democracy,' Fang declared, 'is not something bestowed' (meaning by the CCP).[10] This challenged the legitimacy of the CCP's orthodoxy. When Fang Lizhi began speaking at the student demonstrations in 1986, this had contributed to the reaction by Party traditionalists, and Fang joined Wang Ruoshui in being expelled from the Party in 1987. By 1989, however, others had taken up Fang's and Wang's criticisms and, ominously for the Party traditionalists, many of those intellectuals worked for General Secretary Zhao Ziyang.

Socially, the two greatest unintended consequences for reform were inflation and official corruption. No one really knew exactly how to shift from a planned economy, where prices for inputs or products are set by economists working for the central state, to an economy where those prices are determined by market exchanges. The government experimented with a two-track system for industrial enterprises, where basic production worked under the plan and incentives for extra production, and possible extra profits for the enterprise, worked according to higher market prices. In one sense, this legitimized the 'gray market' for resources that had existed under the plan for years, but the opportunity to exploit the price difference between, say, iron at the plan rate and iron at market rates was too much for many factory managers or local officials to resist. Profiteering was common and obvious to ordinary Chinese, who resented it. But resentment burned to outrage in the face of inflation that cut into the daily lives of urban residents who still lived on fixed work unit (*danwei*) incomes. As Tony Saich has noted, 1989 saw the worst inflation and the most visible official corruption in China since the founding of the PRC.

These were the political and social tensions that led to and defined the Tiananmen demonstrations and military repression. Contingent events – the fateful coming together of Hu Yaobang's death on 15 April, the opportune practice of public funerals for leaders plus the customary spring Qingming festival to honor the dead, and the arrival of international TV crews in May to record the Gorbachev visit – provided the spark to enflame the social resentments over Party corruption and the insecurities of a changing economy (see the Preface, above). Deadlock among the Party leadership over how to handle the demonstrations let this spark become a prairie fire. This invoked the prime directive: never tolerate *luan*. At great cost to his own ambitions for reform, which he knew required stable and open foreign relations, Deng Xiaoping ordered a merciless repression of the public demonstrations and hunted down and punished anyone associated with them.

The world was aghast at what appeared to be the needless brutality of the repression in June 1989. Why use tanks and armored troop carriers to gun down unarmed student demonstrators? China has justifiably been denounced for this state violence. For the historian, the question is why did they do it? Why did Deng imperil his own reforms by this brutal show of power? There are two answers that throw light on present Party policy. First, the political threat of the students was very real. It was a threat to Party legitimacy because of the issue and the advocate. The issue is the Achilles heel of the CCP

– corruption among Party officials. Already in the 1980s, there was popular resentment at the perquisites and personal enrichment of Party functionaries. It was so patently unfair. The students' charges of unfairness echoed resoundingly among the urban population in Beijing and other major cities – similar instances of garnering of economic benefits to themselves were rampant among the local officials. When the students cried 'unfair' (*bu gongping*), the people of Beijing cried back, 'Right!' To make matters worse, the advocates were inheritors of the disproportionate respect in Chinese political culture for the educated. Scholars carry social capital in China. The students knew it; the Party knew it; the urban population believed it. It was a serious contest for public legitimacy. Guns would have been easier for the Party to handle. Given that the Party was already on shaky ground with the public as the implications of Deng's de-Maoification program were still working through and given the serious divisions within the Party leadership over how much reform was enough, this frontal assault on the Party's claim that it was the only possible legitimate public voice of China was very threatening indeed.

What made the threat intolerable was the emerging alliance between the student demonstrators and workers. Informal (and officially illegal) workers' unions were beginning to appear in spring 1989, and they began to support the student demonstrations logistically.[11] To the Party leadership this smelled of a Polish-style Solidarity movement. Moreover, the cardinal rule of CCP power has been never to tolerate alternative forms of political organization. It was the emerging alliance between radical students and workers which was intolerable for Deng Xiaoping. This was for the simple and obvious reason that it was precisely as a union of radical students and working Chinese that the Chinese Communist Party itself had come to power. Added to this deep lesson was the more recent lesson of the Cultural Revolution: student demonstrations had led to *luan* in socialist China. The organizational side of the Tiananmen demonstrations combined with the ideological challenge of 'fairness' (*gongping*) made these teenage activists and their new labor union friends an intolerable threat in the eyes of the CCP leadership. Since 1989, the Party has striven to isolate intellectuals from organizing other social forces (largely by buying the educated elite off with the fruits of globalized markets for the middle class) and has continued to strike hard at any organization that it does not control. This is the root reason for the repression of the Falungong group since 1999, and it was one of the key reasons why Deng Xiaoping struck back with violence in June 1989.

Deng's model: economic reform under Party rule

While the unintended consequences of reform made trouble for Deng Xiaoping's plan of economic openness without political liberalization, the social forces released by the reforms, and in particular the creation of a broader economic elite that derives its wealth from market activity along with varying degrees of privilege within the Party elite, guaranteed the continuation of those plans. In addition to a tiny new tycoon class, Deng's reforms have created a middle class of some 200 million people in China which will not accept a return to the frightening politics and strict government supervision of the Mao era. Just as contingent political events created the greatest crisis of the reform in Tiananmen in 1989, Deng Xiaoping made grand use of his charismatic power in 1992 to cement his reform plan and serve this new social base. Deng's 'Southern Tour' to the Special Economic Zones in South China, and particularly Shenzhen – next to Hong Kong – made it politically impossible for his third successor, General Secretary Jiang Zemin, to turn back. Deng, the last charismatic leader from Mao's revolution, put his authority on the line and his policy in every newspaper: reform and opening are good. Hu Yaobang and Zhao Ziyang were removed from power not because of their reforms but because they failed to oppose bourgeois liberalization appropriately. In a clear message to Party traditionalists, Deng announced that it was now 'leftists' who opposed further reform, and not 'rightists' such as the students of Tiananmen, who presented the greatest challenge for China. The 14th Party Congress in October 1992 relaunched reform, after the post-Tiananmen retrenchment of 1990/91. At the Congress, Jiang Zemin used Deng's authority as a font of Party ideology to certify Deng's 'theory of building socialism with Chinese characteristics,' which amounted to a mix of capitalist economic relations under

Party political control. Further economic reforms were ratified at the Congress under the slogan 'socialist market economy.'

There were reasons beyond Deng Xiaoping's authority for doing so. All leaders in the CCP were shocked by the failed coup attempt in the Soviet Union in 1991. Enough leaders realized that the CCP faced a similar fate unless it could satisfy the material hopes of China's people. Additionally, they realized that the only way to prevent more public demonstrations that could lead to a Chinese Solidarity – or other intellectual–worker or intellectual–farmer alliances – was to provide not only basic economic growth (to absorb a growing workforce) but to make available the fruits of a globalized market, a middle-class existence for energetic and talented students and workers that could distract them all from the absence of political reform. This was Deng Xiaoping's gamble in 1992. It has worked – bringing continued GNP growth and keeping the CCP in power – down to 2006.

This was the watershed for reform China: 1992 is the turning point from which the forces released by the economic and administrative reforms taken by the CCP have built a momentum that cannot be reversed. What they became was a shock to all. What they will become is the challenge before China today. The economic and social success of China's economic reform without political reform contradicts the dominant Western paradigm that links market liberalization with political democratization. That China has followed this contrary model for twenty-five years without the disasters occasioned in the former USSR, Yugoslavia, or contemporary North Korea is worthy of note. While avoiding the suffering of instant neo-liberal reforms – social anomie with ethnic murder or grinding poverty and starvation with increasing popular political/religious fundamentalism – the path of China's reforms has been anything but smooth. The public disaster of the Tiananmen demonstrations and military repression in 1989 was but the most acute instance of the endemic tensions in China's reform program. In short, while China can be credited with undertaking a massive transformation of its economy to fit current global norms which has seen massive and continued growth in GDP without widespread social violence, it is clear that the costs of this economic reform without political reform have been considerable and are growing. The winners need to give back to the system that has allowed them to prosper and the losers are not willing to wait much longer before they are driven back to *luan* to get their basic needs. To understand these pressures, we now turn to look at this brave new world of reform and openness since 1992 to get a sense of the *experience* of those reforms on the ground and across the country.

4 | Brave new world: reform and openness

The experience of reform in China is a story of diversity. It has been widely different for people in different regions or positions in life. China's leaders in the Communist Party may have had the preservation of order (and of their own status) as their primary concern while pursuing national wealth and power through economic reform, but for the bulk of people living in China the experience of reform in the 1980s and 1990s has ranged from a vast improvement of fortunes, through a mixture of opportunity and anxiety, to grinding poverty.

We can picture the social experience of reform in terms of different social places. Different people benefited, were disadvantaged, or were completely unaffected, depending on their region, urban or rural residence, social class, ethnicity or gender. As we have seen in Chapter 3, the first and most spectacular result of the economic reforms was a boom in rural income in the early 1980s. This was followed by increasing troubles in urban industrial communities. Meanwhile, the educated elite thrilled at the new availability of international information, contacts with professional peers, a very few opportunities to visit abroad, and access to more and more news, publications, and programing from around the world. All this was eclipsed by the upheavals around the Tiananmen protests and repression in 1989 and 1990. The next phase began with Deng Xiaoping's famous 1992 Southern Tour, which guaranteed the continuation of the open-door policy and brought a flood of foreign investment. That phase emphatically brought to light the winners and losers of reform, as well as creating the first sustained social contact between large numbers of Hong Kong and Taiwanese businessmen (almost all have been male) and people in both urban and rural China.

All these changes brought a realignment of social classes and social experience in China. In spite of its unitary status and a sense of shared nationality, China is organized into social classes that are effectively segregated from each other in many ways. There are great divides in China today that map out the geographies of winners and losers under reform: coastal provinces versus interior provinces; urban residents versus rural residents; men versus women; Han versus minority groups; and across all these the elite classes versus the ordinary citizen versus the poor. These divides produce social tensions that run through Chinese society like fault lines in the earth – if the pressures build too much and if some 'event' (such as those that triggered the Tiananmen demonstrations of 1989) should strike these faults, then the earthquake of unrest that comes will likely move along one or more of these social fault lines.

This chapter seeks to give a sense of the *experience* of the reforms described in Chapter 3. What actually has happened? What is this brave new world of 'market socialism with Chinese characteristics' like for a range of different Chinese? I present a few concrete examples and people to illustrate the diversity of experience and the role of unintended consequences of reform. The organizing theme for these snapshots from different social groups in China is that with which we began this book: the uneasy coexistence of diverse experience and unified identity. This tension between experience and identity plays out through the fundamental, shared social experience of reform in China: the emergence and sharpening of inequality.

Fantasies of the Western paradise

All that anyone really knew at the start, in the late 1970s, was that things had to change. Urban Chinese were more or less aware that China was well behind the developing Asian economies of Japan, Korea, and Singapore, and many knew that their relatives in Hong Kong and Taiwan enjoyed the comforts of modern industrial society, but almost no one knew just how different things were beyond the social barriers that had sealed off most of Chinese society from the outside world since cold war antagonisms had shut the door in the early 1950s.

Fantasies filled that void. America was the land of gold, Europe the continent of high culture, Japan the Asian miracle. The very few urban Chinese who encountered visiting Western and Japanese students, diplomatic personnel, and the slowly increasing tide of business representatives felt that these people came from a different planet where money and comforts were universal. Taiwanese and Hong Kong 'compatriots' (the PRC name for Chinese in these adjacent territories claimed by the Chinese state but not yet ruled by it) were popularly viewed as the privileged retainers of these foreign rich folk. There has been a marked racial tone to these fantasies. White people were respected, often begrudgingly, for their obvious social and economic success; the Japanese and overseas Chinese were envied; Africans and people from the Middle East were despised for being even poorer than the Chinese. These were fantasies built on the discovery that Maoist propaganda about capitalist exploitation in the West was not true, at least not obviously so. The first reaction was to assume that the opposite had to be true: that everything was beautiful in the West. Even the most patriotic North American or European students studying in China were embarrassed and felt obliged to point out that their society was not so perfect.[1]

These idealized images would pass as urban Chinese and university students began to study in North America, Europe, and Australia. By the late 1980s tens of thousands were living modestly in university towns in the West and many were working in low-paying jobs with no benefits (as illegal workers); the bloom was off the Western rose. This contributed to the rising popular nationalism of the 1990s that has been driven by the middle class most attuned to these overseas student experiences. Geremie Barmé gives a lurid example of this:

> In *A Beijing Man in New York*, China's most popular 1993 television series, the protagonist Wang Qingming, a man on his way to making a fortune after a train of failures and betrayals, gets himself a local American prostitute. She is white, blond, and buxom. Wang decides to take out his frustrations on the hired help. While thrusting himself into the prostrate sex worker, Wang showers her with dollar bills ... [demanding] she cry out repeatedly: 'I love you, I love you.'[2]

Barmé's point is that this tasteless bit of imagined reality TV was, according to at least one Chinese review, a particularly popular scene from the series. It captured the angry populism of urban China in the 1990s, reactions to American and European smugness over Tiananmen, the experience of racism in those countries by Chinese students, and the beginnings of confidence among China's emerging middle class.

In the countryside, images of the West were more vague, as very few non-Chinese visited China's vast range of rural communities and regional cities in the 1980s. Encounters with the West came to these areas later and by proxy. They came with the expansion of television and in the last decade satellite TV into every county and nearly every household in China. People in Western societies forget that even today, in 2006, most Chinese have never met a foreigner; but most have seen any number of (dubbed) Hollywood sitcoms, Taiwan historical dramas, Hong Kong fashion shows, or Korean dramas.[3]

These images form a key backdrop to the direct and visceral experience of individuals and communities as they live out the reform policies unleashed by Deng Xiaoping. Naturally, it is their social experience, more than images of the foreign world, which has defined the identity and interests of various people in China. The divergence of experience, particularly between the privileged urban and east coast professional classes and the rural and poor in the interior provinces, is vast. And yet nearly all maintain an identity as Chinese, or at least as citizens of China. The exceptions are the Tibetans, some Muslims, and minorities associated with neighboring countries (Central Asia, Mongolia, Korea, and Vietnam). But it is astonishing that such a diverse range of peoples holds to this shared identity. Part of the reason is the shared contrast with Western experience, particularly as portrayed on the now ubiquitous TV. Ironically, access to a moderate range of commercial entertainment programing from Western societies on Chinese TV has reinforced a shared Chinese national identity.

Boom and bust on the farm

The split between urban and rural life in China did not start with the post-Mao reforms. The great divergence in living standards and social identity between town and country emerged with China's integration into the world capitalist system in the nineteenth century.

Before then, relative wealth was less a matter of urban or rural residency than one of living in a prosperous area or era or not. Cultural norms and lifeways were more consistent across rural and urban communities in great part because the elite, the scholar-official class, served in the city but grew up in and retired to their lands in the countryside. Today we generally refer to these traditional values as 'Confucian,' but in fact they were a working mix of the philosophy of Confucius himself, as well as norms and practices from Mahayana Buddhism and Daoism. These ideas were shared across classes because there was regular contact between those classes – largely as landlord and tenants. This rural-urban system underwrote a reasonably stable patriarchal and commercial society with strong communitarian goals.[4] Industrialization and increased contact with European merchants, missionaries, and diplomats brought changes in economic and ideational life that we associate with an urban culture that is 'modern' and a rural culture that is 'backward.' By the 1920s, the reformist intelligentsia of treaty-port cities, such as Shanghai and Canton (Guangzhou), as well as Beijing, identified with science, democracy, and industrial society and worried about the backward nature of China's rural masses. A generation before, those same masses had been viewed by Confucian scholar-officials not as unmodern but simply as poorer than in earlier times.

Socialist development under the CCP only cemented these new economic and cultural divides, despite Mao's much-publicized emphasis on 'learning from the workers, peasants, and soldiers.' Mao's Great Leap Forward in 1958 was predicated on a utopian image of this non-urban culture of the peasantry, one that was shared neither by urban nor, ironically, rural inhabitants. Indeed, the Great Leap institutionalized the *hukou* internal passport system that effectively re-enfeudalized the peasantry and locked them on the land and out of the commercial and industrial cities.[5] Mao used this de jure nobility of the peasantry and de facto territorial bondage of rural residency to defuse the chaos of the early Cultural Revolution. In 1968 the CCP began to rusticate (*xiafang*) rebellious Red Guard youth to the countryside 'to learn from the peasants.' Many youth believed and went voluntarily, others less so, but in the end millions of urban youths were 'sent down.'[6]

The experience of these 17 million sent-down youths (*zhiqing*) plays a central role in reform China. The experience was unpleasant for all (including, let us not forget, the rural residents who had to cope with these imported youths), traumatic for many, and fatal for some. The profound economic and social backwardness of rural China in the 1960s stunned these urban socialist youths. Often without electricity, not to mention the schools, medical services and entertainments of the city, these rural communities did not in the main welcome these strangers, who lacked local knowledge or farm skills. In addition, many of the youths were subject to the abuse and sexual depredations of local leaders who felt that kids with no clan or lineage connections could hardly complain. The survivors clawed their way back to urban China in the mid- and late 1970s. The experience has marked them for life. The exceptional did well and lead in university, government, and business life today, but they carry the memory of the poverty and ill governance in rural China. Wei Jingsheng, of 1979 Democracy Wall fame (Chapter 3, above), is but one of many democracy advocates and reformers in China to come from this group. The less gifted or fortunate have become 'the forgotten generation,' denied an education and made superfluous in China's new knowledge-driven economy, which generates in excess of 15 million high school graduates a year with more training than these old Red Guards. This forgotten generation forms a potential cadre of reaction to reform. Toughened by their own experience, they know how to rebel against authorities and they have a keen nose for injustice.

China's reforms began by addressing these cleavages but in the end have only built on them. Today, the divergence between urban and rural China has only gotten worse. Broadly speaking, per capita income between 1988 and 1995 grew twice as fast for urban residents as for rural. The average income for urban Shanghai in 1999 was over 8,000 yuan (about $US1,000) while in rural Gansu it is 1,400 (or $175).[7] The income gap has only grown in recent years. Yet Deng Xiaoping's reforms began in the countryside with the decollectivization of farmland. Called the household responsibility system, this breaking up of the communes had begun in 1979 as farmers in poor areas simply divided up communal land on their own. By 1982 the new PRC State Constitution moved the political and administrative powers of the 55,000 communes to 96,000 revived townships and the Party enforced a standardized version of decollectivization. By 1984 cropping contracts to individual farm families were being guaranteed for fifteen years, and they had been extended to fifty years by the 1990s.[8] This allowed farming families to make their own farming choices and to engage in sideline production. Private markets were once again tolerated. At the same time, the state subsidized agriculture by spending over 1 billion yuan (US$125 million) to keep the price of grain up for farmers but down for urban consumers.

While the promise of markets brought welcome opportunity to rural families, it was the state subsidies and broader market forces which determined the slide back into poverty for much of rural China. By 1984 the state could no longer afford the subsidies for grain and so ended mandatory purchases. The price of rice fell, along with that of other staples, and rural communities that had seen a burst of wealth – and new construction – in recent years now came upon hard times. New production quotas for grain were introduced at low prices (which the state could afford). The net result was that many farmers quit farming, or limited it to subsistence, and stalked off to the cities to try their luck. Throughout the 1990s this migrant labour, now a 'floating population' of 150 million, defined both urban life and the rural communities to which it sent remittances. Back on the farm women, children, and the aged carry on; in the working slums of reform China men earn wages, endure the sojourner's life, and bring back images of the big city along, too often, with STDs.

What does 'life on the farm' look like in China today? While experiences vary, Susan Blum gives a compelling composite picture of the poverty and feminization of agriculture that characterizes much of rural life:

> A 45-year-old woman, performing agricultural and domestic tasks for her family while her husband and son are in the county seat trying to earn some money, and she and her daughter-in-law try to manufacture some small items, produce their requisite amount of grain, raise pigs, chickens, and ducks, embroider, watch the two

children, saving money for taxes and education and health care ...
Maybe her mother-in-law, 67, has a broken hip. There is no money
to spare for her treatment, so they just try to give her broth ... Some
houses in the hamlet even have electricity. There they can all watch
TV in the evening, doing mending by its dim light.[9]

While the abuses of local officials and thugs are real, many of the
problems in rural China are communal and stem from the legacies
of land distribution under Mao. Astonishingly, there has not been
a proper land survey in China. Chinese law says rural land belongs
to the village as a corporate entity. During the Mao period, county
administrations, or in the 1960s commune administrations, could
requisition this village land for public uses – dams, rural enterprises,
a pig farm. An unintended consequence of the decollectivization in
the 1980s was to put these earlier transactions back on the table
for negotiation – because it was unclear which village would now
own the dam, the workshop or the pig farm. China's legal system
is not yet up to the task of adjudicating these myriad community
land claims. Yet there is progress. Not only has the central state
enacted new laws, such as the 1998 Revised Land Administration
Law, but scholarly circles have publicized (albeit in the limited realm
of academic journals) examples of land cases and their arbitration
in the journal *Democracy and Law*, reflecting modest improvements
in this key arena of economic governance based in no small part on
the pressures that rural collective action by farmers have brought
to bear.[10]

China's reforms began essentially with the neo-liberal promise
that privatization and an open market would bring prosperity to rural
China. As has been the case elsewhere, the market alone has not
been able to deliver such economic dynamism with equity. Realities
of institutional heritage (the tangle of land claims from Mao's communes), price supports (and their removal), and gendered access to
work in the cities had far more impact on most rural Chinese than
the small number of market gardeners in the suburbs of big cities
who made small fortunes. The rural experience of reform has been
that the market has helped, but the market alone is not enough,
and the market alone can be disastrous for many.

Trouble in town

Urban reform started later and moved more hesitantly but has, in the end, taken the lead. The core issue of urban China has been the *danwei* or work unit of the state-owned enterprise (SOE). This extends from service industries such as banks, universities, department stores, and administrative units to heavy industry. As we saw in Chapter 1, work units provided not only employment but residence, healthcare, and a range of other social services. Thus, restructuring industrial China has been a more complex issue than decollectivizing the land. It has been a long and bumpy transition. It began with efforts to bring accountability for profits and losses to the existing SOEs by giving managers more freedom to choose but more responsibility for covering losses. Increasing percentages of profits were allowed to be retained by these units in exchange for increasing responsibility to pay off their own debts. As the 1980s progressed, the results were mixed, and by 1989 there were real social tensions stemming from the urban reform effort. The key problem in urban reform was the move from plan to market – how was one to determine the cost of something when there had not been a commercial market in China for decades? This left much room for official malfeasance, expropriation and profiteering from the difference between the low plan price of an input (say iron ore) and the higher market price. This dual-track pricing was intended to bridge the transition from plan to market. The result was very bad inflation by 1988. This hammered urban residents, most of whom were on fixed incomes. Urban anger was exacerbated by widespread official corruption, which seemed much worse than even during the Cultural Revolution. These two pressures provided the urban fuel for the explosion of student demonstrations in Tiananmen in the spring of 1989.

State reforms in the 1990s, particularly after Deng Xiaoping's famous reaffirmation of economic reform in his January and February 1992 'Southern Tour,' addressed just these issues. The 14th Party Congress of 1992 legislated this commitment to reform in the name of 'socialist market economy' based on the 'theory of building socialism with Chinese characteristics.' Intellectuals chuckled then at this euphemism for capitalist practice under the CCP – just as they do today at Jiang Zemin's 'Three Represents' policy, which has welcomed capitalists into the CCP since 2002 – but the ideological formulations allowed the CCP to carry out what has been the single most successful reform of a state socialist economy anywhere in the world. In fact, the blueprint for the current reforms had been put forward in 1986 by Zhao Ziyang, but it took more than a decade to get workable details on paper and through the bureaucratic wrangles in Beijing. The application of the model was put forward by Premier Zhu Rongji at the 9th NPC Congress in March 1998. It covers all the right things: a national grain market to balance guaranteed food supply and farmers' income; overhaul of the financial system, especially China's troubled state banks; marketization of housing; medical care reform; and rationalization of the tax system.[11]

What has come out of the reforms is a new urban China. The glitz and energy of Pudong in Shanghai, the forest of new skyscrapers in Beijing, and the endless traffic of all these cities and a dozen more from Chongqing to Guangzhou to Tianjin have grown under these reforms, which have allowed the shifting of state assets in the SOEs to the market and have induced unprecedented amounts of foreign direct investment (FDI), as we shall see below. At the same time as a newly entitled middle class has emerged, a dispossessed class of former SOE workers who have been put out of work and denied their rightful pensions broods, and an underclass of migrant workers jostle in the streets of these cities.

The life of a middle-class professor and of a rural migrant capture this dichotomy of urban life in China today. In the suburbs of Shanghai, a successful tenured professor at a major university enjoys his new town house and car with his wife, an editor at a local press, and their pre-teen son. The housing development is clean and modern and looks like any medium-density, middle-class residential area in Europe. It is a fair way out in the suburbs, but Shanghai's mass transit serves our professor well enough. The house is spacious (three bedrooms, etc., comprising some 1,500 square feet). It has a pleasant pocket garden in the back which sports a grille and, on the third floor, our professor's pride and joy – nearly twenty shelves of books in the study. While he enjoys the fruits of academic success, our professor worries how the inequalities he sees all around Shanghai can be addressed. His approach is to work with fellow academics and unofficial intellectuals (that is, those who earn their money from business rather than universities) to discuss China's social problems and policy solutions. They write papers and run a webpage. When even these few urban intellectuals try to concern themselves with the problems of social inequality, however, they immediately bump into the Party's ban on political discourse outside Party channels. As of 2006 our Shanghai academic cannot publish or give public talks in Shanghai and has been sent off to the Central Party School for a month of re-education. This is not a repeat of Mao's humiliation of intellectuals, much less a gulag terror, but the Party's anxious interventions have not helped to mobilize the talents of China's well-to-do to address the problems of reform.

At the same time in downtown Beijing at the 'people market' outside Dongdan Park in the center of the city, itinerant workers gather each morning to look for work. Sang Ye interviewed one from Jianli, Hubei province. He leads a handful of buddies in his village to hop a train to get work in Guangzhou, in southern China, but after a day on the goods train, it gets colder: they've hopped the wrong train and end up in Beijing. His first job is as an internal wetback labourer in a small restaurant, working around the clock for about 100 to 130 RMB a month (US$8–10). 'Most restaurant workers earn about that much,' he says. 'It's a hard job, and the bosses are pretty much the same, though they have to cope with all the worries and work harder than we do. ... Back in Jianli I wouldn't make a hundred Yuan in a year, let alone in a month.' He bounces between jobs, gets ripped off by labor foremen and has to endure sexual advances from a trucking boss, but nonetheless he is able to return home with 2,500 RMB to share with his parents. When Sang Ye interviewed him, he had returned with his young nephew for the next round. The young man had come to look for work because of the poverty of his home village. Tough and practical, this migrant worker had his own views: 'The people in the old Communist areas made much greater contributions to the revolution than city people. So many lives were lost; the Communists had grown to strength and then came to power on the backs of people like us. But after he went to Beijing, even Chairman Mao didn't do anything for us, let alone Chairman Hua. Sure, they spoke about the victory of the revolution, but we were still as dirt poor as we had been in the old society.'[12] The young man's story, however, does not focus on class politics, but on the grim chances of survival.

The social life of joint ventures

The major engine of growth has been FDI. Absolutely staggering amounts of foreign investment have come into China over the past thirty years, and especially in the past fifteen years since the water-shed year of 1992. Since 2000 foreign direct investment in China had averaged nearly US$50 billion each year, with $115 billion contracted for 2003 and $53 billion already spent for that year.[13] Joint ventures began cautiously in the 1980s, but have opened up in the 1990s, and now wholly owned foreign enterprises are allowed in China. These economic entities have changed the working life of China, as well as contributing to the consumer choice available to those Chinese with the means to shop beyond necessities. The transformation of the Chinese work unit has first and foremost been based on working for Hong Kong- and Taiwanese-invested businesses. European and American investments are much smaller by comparison. All comport to some fashion of modern capitalist management.

By the late 1990s the worst industrial work conditions were in foreign-invested factories in South China. These sweatshops were run by Hong Kong, Taiwan, and Korean businessmen. The New York-based NGO National Labor Committee made an extended study of the conditions and the complicity of major Western brand-name clothing manufacturers in particular. For example, at Kang Yi Fashion Manufacturers in Shenzhen, which makes clothing for Ann Taylor and Preview, 'three hundred women work fourteen hours a day, six days a week, at wages that range from 14 to 23 cents an hour.' Even that pitiful wage was often paid weeks late. Working conditions were cramped and unsafe, lacking fire exits. This labor regime, concludes Tim Weston, 'amounts to indentured servitude.'[14] The official trade union, the All-China Federation of Trade Unions, is the only legal representation the workers here – or in any factory in China – can have. It is, sadly, deeply compromised. Often the local representative for the ACFTU is a relative of the factory owner. International pressure, as in the campaign against Nike, has helped a bit, but the continuing labor revolts (see Chapter 5) indicate that social justice for labor in China is a battle yet to be won.

Joint ventures, like other businesses and factories in China, operate under the seductive labor conditions offered by the huge 'floating population' of migrant labor. This nation of lumpenproletariat lacks the basic citizenship rights of other urban residents. They do not have urban *hukou* status, and so not only do they lack social services support, including access to education for their children, but also they cannot bargain with their employers. A recent study comparing post-socialist labor reform in Vietnam and China highlights the residual damage of the *hukou* residential permit system. Vietnam's *doimoi* reforms are in many ways similar to the 'market socialism' of China, yet workers in Vietnam's joint venture factories fare much better than Chinese laborers. The key difference: the Vietnamese workers 'belong' to the communities in which they work and have better support from their labor unions and even local government. The Vietnamese example shows that the abuse of migrant labor in China is not a *necessary* phase in the transition to a market economy.[15] Yet, as with the day laborer from Hunan we met above, joint venture workers focus not on these macro-structural factors, but on survival on a daily basis and on violent resistance when it all becomes too much.

Gendered reform and the generation gap

Underlying both the rural and urban transitions to market socialism, or authoritarian capitalism, is a profound gender divide. The experience of women, now slightly less than half of the population, is widely different from that of men, and most often more difficult. In rural China, the shift away from Maoist egalitarian ideology has seen a shameless resurgence of patriarchal familial norms. These are reinforced by gender demarcations in employment. In the countryside, young girls are married out to their in-laws' homes, to serve husband and mother-in-law, and are left on the farm to raise children, care for aged parents of their husbands, and farm while the husband goes to town – the local township or regional city or even

Shanghai – to earn cash. The benefits of reform, such as they are, for rural residents disproportionately redound to the male members of the clan.

The pressures of the newly uncertain life in the countryside include the state family planning policy of one child per couple, or at most two. This has occasioned increased abortion of female fetuses and even female infanticide if a male child has not been produced within the quota. One result of the gendered inequalities of rural life has been a marked increase in female suicide – to protest against arranged marriages, abusive husbands, or grinding poverty.[16] While the natural gender ratio at birth is 95 girls per 100 boys, China's average in 2002 was 86 girls per 100 boys. Since the introduction of the one-child policy in 1980 this has produced a shortage of women of marriageable age and, according to UNICEF, has contributed to the trafficking (kidnap and sale) of some 250,000 women and children in 2003.[17]

The skewed gender ratio has contributed to a new social world for young Chinese. In Shanghai, for example, young educated women – with that all-important Shanghai *hukou* residence status – ironically enjoy a favored life. I remember watching with amazement at a self-service restaurant in Shanghai in the 1990s as a husband of a young family tended to his wife and single child, carrying food and cleaning up in the style of a compliant wife. When I commented on this to my Chinese colleague, she chuckled and said, 'Hey, there's fifteen guys waiting in line to take his place. If he doesn't like it, he can move along.' Indeed, family life has changed dramatically for urban households over the past fifteen years. The one-child policy has produced a generation of 'singletons' – Chinese born and raised without siblings but with relatively better-off parents *and* four doting grandparents. Along with the discrediting of Maoist ideals of public service, the socialization of singletons creates a Chinese version of 'bowling alone.' Showered with toys and computers, but expected to excel at school, both boys and girls live in air-conditioned isolation, where common activities are limited to school, shopping, and perhaps a bit of basketball. The world of this new singleton generation is the Internet.

Young China in the urban middle classes is characterized by

these two social facts: the singleton kid and life on the Web. China's Internet is the biggest in the world, whether one counts number of users writing in Chinese, hours spent online, or volume of traffic. In short order the major language of the Internet – the language of the greatest number of messages – will be Chinese. While older Chinese cruise webpages and order tickets online while sending a few e-mails, China's urban youth live on the Web. Most hours are spent in video-gaming, interactive fantasy or quest contests, or diverting aracade-style shoot'-em-ups. To walk into a public Web bar in urban China – including, increasingly, smaller regional cities and large county towns – is to crash into the clamour of a video arcade. This is bowling alone with Chinese characteristics.

Yet life online is not merely or only an alienating distraction. The political space that the Web provides in bulletin boards, blogs, and online chat-rooms and journal webpages is very real in China. Indeed, it is the main focus of the efforts of the Chinese state to monitor and control the Internet in China. It is domestic speech, particularly young Chinese who criticize the government for being 'soft on America' and 'not defending China's dignity against Japan,' and not BBC or Fox News reports, which predominantly concern China's Public Security Bureau (the national police). And well they should pay attention to this youth talk. China's students form the cutting edge of nationalistic talk. Predominantly male and between eighteen and twenty-five years old, this online community takes the living Maoism and defensive nationalism of the Party leadership to places Beijing would rather not go. These youths revere Mao because they believe he lived simply and thus was not corrupt. Moreover, they take the radical populism in Maoism to heart. Slogans such as 'Serve the people' and 'Leadership of the working class,' which make their elders (as survivors of the Cultural Revolution) gag, inspire these youths, who never knew the political terror of those years but do know street beggars, shantytowns, and TV images of rural poverty. As they sit alone in the glow of their computer screens, Maoist talk gives these modern youths a sense of purpose and intimations of community. In truth, they no more understand the lives of rural women or sweatshop workers than they do those of ethnic communities across China. They are strangers to these other Chinese, and despite brave Maoist talk, the urban youths share their parents' anxiety about reform.

Ethnic reform

Reform has not been the same for China's 100 million 'national minorities.' In Xinjiang, young Muslim Uighurs endure unemployment and hang out listening to tapes of Islamic lectures, music from the Stans (what are now the Central Asian republics of Kazakhstan, Kyrghyzstan, etc.), and political comedy. In Yunnan province, some minority counties have received so much supplementary support from the government that they have developed a form of welfare dependency. Xiaolin Guo's research in northern Yunnan turns up the contrary case in which a few years after the central government started paying subsidies to 'poverty counties' the number of such counties increased – as there was little incentive to pull oneself out of the poverty classification. When the local state is staffed by minorities, intra-ethnic tensions surface, as in the case of Dai areas considered by Tony Saich, mentioned in Chapter 1. In Songpan county in northwest Sichuan, Jack Hayes found that Tibetan herders and mountain people did not so much resent the Han government officials as loathe the newly arrived Hui merchants and middlemen. Here the lines of ethnic community organized economic reform, as one, then another ethnic group came to dominate herding, forestry, local commerce, and the all-important new resource: tourism. Unlike the urban youth and rural poor or working-class versus middle-class women, these communities know each other because they live in the same geographic and social space. Competition, rather than alienation, defines their relations.[18] In northwest Sichuan, the Tibetan herders and farmers see the Hui shopkeepers as lying, cheating merchants who connive with the Han officials to defraud poor Tibetans. The Hui see the Tibetans as lazy, careless of natural resources, and prone to violence. The Han officials see the Tibetans as a problem to be handled and the Hui as unreliable allies in state efforts to 'develop' the region. In each case, ethnic communities struggle to find a way to do better under the shifting rules of engagement of the CCP's reform policies.

Elite, middle class, and the poor

Class is back in China. As one academic intellectual quipped recently, 'Under Mao when we were all pretty much as poor as each other, we always talked about class struggle. Now that there really are distinct economic classes in China, we can't talk about class struggle anymore.' Reform in China has seen an astonishingly quick and brutal return to extreme class divisions. While GDP has gone up impressively at an annual rate of 8–10 percent per year since the 1980s, and there is more actual production of wealth in China's economy, the distribution of that wealth has been sharply skewed. There is now a small but fabulously wealthy elite, a middle class of about 200 million, a broad middle of some 800 to 900 million who strive to get by and hope for a better future, and at least 200 million bitterly poor. Among that lower three-quarters of Chinese are the 150 million floating population of migrant workers.

The rich The past fifteen years have been a wonderful time for China's top elite. They have prospered as never before, amassing great wealth, directing major business empires, building a life of comfort and conspicuous consumption. This top elite, naturally enough, is tiny. It is composed of a very few from the top Party circles, quite often the sons and daughters of a top leader known as 'princelings,' and a very few entrepreneurs who have done well, often hand in hand with the princelings. These are the glitzy examples profiled in the Western press, sporting their BMWs, villas in gated communities, and overseas investments. All this is relatively open, if widely resented by other classes, though it is not clear to what extent organized crime – in the form of drug and prostitution traffic – plays a role. Certainly, the narco culture that bedevils life in Latin America is not, as yet, a major influence in Chinese society.

Deng Xiaoping declared that 'to get rich is glorious,' hoping that the trickle-down effect of a new class of economic winners would boost China's economy. This policy dovetails with long-held social norms that recognize and honour financial success. The most vivid example of this privileging of wealth is the automobile. China's streets are a battlefield of hierarchy. The most dangerous thing for a visitor from Europe or North America is to cross the street in

Beijing or Guangzhou at a pedestrian crossing. Cars have the right of way, always. Local residents chuckle when questioned about this: 'Well, they have enough money to buy a car and they're damned well going to use it.' The uglier side of this conspicuous display is traffic accidents. There are endless stories of pedestrians killed by drivers who either simply race off or, even if brought to court, get off with minor fines. A gruesome story emerged in 2006. A driver of an expensive imported car ran over an old woman when backing out of a parking space in a downtown garage. The security camera caught the macabre spectacle: the driver didn't hop out to see whether the pedestrian was still alive, but rather drove forward and reversed again over the body – clearly to ensure the victim was dead. Why does this behavior make sense? Because it is cheaper to pay the surviving family members for an 'accidental death' than to support a disabled person.

The middle class China has a middle class of some 200 million people, that is, people who can afford to invest in an apartment and education for their children, buy or aspire to buy a car, and consume those things that signify success in China today – clothes, restaurant meals, shopping in general, and family vacations, including to international destinations such as Thailand and Europe.

As we saw in the example of our Shanghai professor's family, this class is busy and largely apolitical, though pollution, popular nationalism, and fear of the ragged migrant workers in their urban neighborhoods, and finally run-ins with corrupt or unresponsive local government offices, pull middle-class Chinese into the public arena. Like the political elite, they fear *luan* and wish to hang on to and, to the degree possible, extend the benefits they have enjoyed from reform. We might best imagine the lives of the middle class in two forms: ordinary life and extraordinary circumstances. In ordinary life, the attention of a middle-class urban Chinese is focused on the nuclear family, able to live without grandparents or adult siblings because of the boom in the housing market and increased urban incomes. The norm is husband and wife, both working, and one child, with at least one set of grandparents near by. Attention is divided between the adult couple and their interests and the cultivation of the golden child. The life of the child is full and strangely passive. The doting parents and grandparents ply the child with food, clothes, toys, presents, and attention. The child's duty is to study and excel at school and to get into a prestigious university. The parents find new opportunities to enjoy each other's company, particularly while consuming the treats of urban life, from shopping to dining to vacations. As is true of most humans, the increased leisure enjoyed by middle-class couples has also been used to indulge in self-focused pleasures, from harmless entertainments to marital affairs.

The working class Working-class life is hard in China today. While urban workers enjoy the street culture, films, shopping and general bustle of China's vibrant commercial districts, work has changed from the drab but secure world of the *danwei*. At minimum, most workers no longer enjoy the lifelong employment of the old work units and have little trust in enterprise pensions. Wages are good, however, and smart working-class families salt money away for a rainy day.

Working-class life has been dominated by two major changes in reform China: layoffs and unemployment stemming from the reform of SOEs and the influx of 'cheap labor' in the form of China's burgeoning internal migrant population. For families of middle-aged workers in SOEs that have downsized or gone bust, this is a disaster. Urban unemployment in China is disguised by the practice of *xiagang* (off duty), in which workers in a state-owned enterprise are maintained on the rolls but do not work and receive only a token welfare payment (not nearly enough to live on). Xiagang workers must then compete in a depressed labor market swamped with rural migrants. Younger workers retrain, start selling in the street markets, move along. Older workers, in their fifties, suffer particularly. Their skills are not wanted in the service sector and they have been made redundant in the industrial sector. By the late 1990s there were at least 20 million such destitute workers nationwide.[19]

Mindful of a better life before and of their official high status under Mao as the proletariat, this social group provides the rank and file for an urban uprising – if given leadership. Already, workers have acted across China in thousands of demonstrations aimed at recovering their jobs, their pensions, their rights to subsistence. An example is the protest held by workers in the Chongqing Knitting Mill in November 1992. As has been the case with so many similar protests across China in the 1990s, this action was based on the moral claims of a right to subsistence – in this case pensions for retired workers. When this large stated-owned enterprise went bankrupt it cut back on pension payments to retired workers. Retirees and current workers took to the street, pleading their case to riot police. They argued in a language all understood: their pension payment was their rightful part of the surplus value they had generated for the state as workers in the factory. It was *unfair* for the enterprise to keep back their repayment. Current workers, unsurprisingly, took the opportunity to demand state assurances that they, too, would be guaranteed their basic right to live. After five days of confrontation, the local authorities accepted the workers' demands: pensions would not be cut; current workers would be retained or assigned to similar work.[20] This pattern has been repeated literally thousands of times across China, and constitutes the current method of handling worker discontent: so long as the demonstrations are local and the problem clear cut, the Party pays; as soon as cross-regional or cross-class associations form, the Party cracks down.

The underclass A miserable underclass of migrant workers now plies the highways of rural China and haunts the urban paradises they help build. In 2006 this 'floating population' is estimated to be 150 million people.[21] These are largely rural workers, almost all men, who leave their families and farms in the countryside to seek relatively better-paying labor in medium to large cities. They provide the necessary labor for the mammoth construction boom that defines China's cities today. As a result of the *hukou* system, however, they do not have what Dorothy Solinger calls 'citizenship rights' in their place of work. They cannot bring their families, educate their children, or press their rights to fair treatment, payment for their labor and protection from abuse by police and officials. These are the sweatshop workers of China's joint venture factories. As we saw in the case of the migrant laborer from Hubei, for all the suffering of migrant workers in the cities, the economic impact of their labor in their home counties is substantial. Internal remittances form a major part of the income for poorer counties and villages, and the social consequences of absent fathers and brothers run deep.[22]

In all, the worlds of the rich, the middle classes, and the poor highlight the social consequences of the huge gap between the winners and losers of reform: Chinese society has been carved up into mutually alienated communities by social class, as well as by region, gender, and ethnicity. The rich fear the poor, the poor resent their fate, the middle classes want to keep order. The Party keeps that order but has not been able to address sufficiently the fears, resentments, or desires of China's fragmented population. As was the case throughout the twentieth century, many in China turn for help to the inheritors of the mantle of Confucius and the scholar-officials: China's intellectuals.

Liberty and anxiety for intellectuals

Intellectuals in China are a tiny minority, but a disproportionately influential one in government, business, and media. They are also a major source of information about and analysis of Chinese society. What we know of China largely comes through the prism of China's intellectuals, academics, specialists, and media leaders. While Western academics and journalists have focused on the handful of courageous dissidents who have challenged the CCP and generally suffered the consequences, the vast majority of intellectuals in China try to work within the system.[23] While the public arena has opened tremendously in the 1990s, and public intellectuals need not be in or speak for the Party, Party control remains an important bedrock of contemporary China. If one crosses into the areas proscribed by the Party (such as Falungong, Taiwan, or Tibetan independence, or criticizing CCP leaders by name), the Party can and does exercise quick and decisive repression.

Intellectual life in China has bloomed, but many intellectuals fear they have become hothouse flowers for the enjoyment of the rich and powerful. Intellectuals in China are variously defined, but if we take college-educated people as a general indicator, that would be some 45 million people in 2000 or about 4 percent of the population (and indeed, two-thirds of this tiny number hold two-year certificates rather than full four-year degrees).[24]

At whatever level, China's intellectuals deal with the social consequences of reform. According to one Beijing commentator:

> I fear no social group has had such ups and downs as intellectuals have, experiencing such a dramatic fate in a century of profound changes: from heroes of creation to objects of remolding, from subjects of discourse to marginal mayflies ... They created myths and were shattered by those myths; they led the currents and were engulfed by those currents.[25]

This passage reflects the concerns uppermost in the minds of China's thinkers and writers today: what should intellectuals do? It also asks a question that could not be more alien to Western media reports. China's intellectuals have been, and continue to be, presented in the *New York Times* and *Le Monde* as anti-communist heroes. Yet this gap between Chinese experience and Western image has closed in scholarly writing. Not only have the questions that animate those born and raised in Western societies changed, but also many Chinese intellectuals have joined the ranks of Western university professors and academic writers. Thus, our picture of China's intellectuals today describes not only the increasing impact of transnational market forces and media interests in China but also the impact of Chinese scholars now active in Western universities.[26]

The most important impact of reform for China's intellectuals has been the 'disestablishment' of China's intellectuals from the Party-State and the opening of a confusing array of overlapping alternative roles to play. As the CCP has withdrawn from its totalitarian goal of controlling all of society as it did under Mao and has, instead, embraced 'market socialism,' it has ended the intellectuals' role as public officials. The price of today's relative autonomy for China's intellectuals has been a loss of public influence and the birth of the self-doubt and questioning we saw in Zhu Yong's quote, above. The reforms have brought on the *disaggregation of intellectuals* in China – no longer will a Wang Ruoshui or a Fang Lizhi (heroes of reform in the 1980s) stand for all China's intellectuals. We now regularly see a range of intellectual roles – creative writers, artists, journalists, academics, scientists, technical government or business advisors. This has paralleled the *disaggregation of the Establishment*. The state, that is the Party-State under the CCP, is still very much with us. Just ask any Chinese academic. Nonetheless, the authority of the state is more than matched, on a day-to-day level, by the requirements of professions (universities, institutes, businesses), the interests of local governments, and the financial inducements of commercial publishing.

Professions, the Party, and the public are the three masters to whom Chinese intellectuals must bow if they are to survive and be effective in their chosen goals. A few examples will give a sense of Chinese intellectuals with global characteristics since the 1990s. Consider the plight of Liu Dong, editor of *China Academics* (*Zhongguo xueshu*) and Professor of Comparative Literature at Beijing University. Unlike intellectuals under Mao who had to please their Party secretary and keep on the right side of the Great Helmsman while pursuing their ideals of socialist service, Professor Liu faces a more complex world. He must not only demonstrate his academic abilities to his peers (at Harvard, the co-publisher of his journal, as well as his own university), but he must also satisfy market forces or his journal will go under. Nonetheless, he must still keep on the right side of his Party secretary, pay for his cell phone, and take care of his kids' education costs. How does he get his funding? How does he get published? What can he hope his writings will achieve in political or public influence? How will he balance the specialist demands of his academic peers with the commercial interests of an emerging middle-class readership?

He has, of course, new tools: the Internet, Harvard-Yenching funding, that cell phone.[27] These pressures are familiar to academics in the West, but Liu Dong's conditions are meaningfully different: the Party still rules and China's economic reforms have everywhere brought social ills of rural poverty, urban homelessness, and pollution that are far more intense and urgent than in Western societies. What does Professor Liu Dong do with these international resources? He declares the fundamental power of *place* (or location) in scholarship. He denounces Chinese scholars who ape Western ways as 'pidgin scholarship.'[28] He is a most interesting character: a cosmopolitan academic with strong international connections, who specializes in German literary history and theory, and yet accepts that his place – living and working in China – defines what he should do: serve China according to his best lights as an intellectual.

Meanwhile, in Shanghai, Xu Jilin, Professor of History at East China Normal University, has staked a reputation as one of the most prolific public intellectuals and academics in China today. He's published nearly a dozen books, appears regularly in the highbrow PRC intellectual press, such as *Reading* (*Dushu*), or influential Web journals, such as *21st Century* (*Ershiyi shiji*) and intellectual webpages such as *Shiji Zhongguo* (Century China).[29] He is much more interested in Western ideas for China, particularly the political philosophy of liberalism – which he takes to be social democracy – than is Liu Dong.[30] Yet he has traveled and studied in the West much less than Liu. This has not stopped Professor Xu from spending six months as a visiting scholar at Harvard-Yenching in 2001 or from organizing conferences with Western colleagues.[31]

The disaggregation of Chinese intellectuals today also raises the question: when is a Chinese intellectual Chinese and when does one become foreign? This is part of the globalization that confounds scholars in China and in Western societies. This confusion arises particularly as Chinese scholars receive graduate training in the West, take up academic posts in America or Europe and publish in English, fully engaging with the scholarly discourse in Western academia. By 2006, literally thousands of Chinese students had joined the academy in the West; among them several study China's intellectuals.[32]

A good example of this globalized hybrid is Professor Zhang Xudong. He is a very important example of contemporary Chinese life – because he is a professor of Literature and Asian Studies at NYU. He is also an adjunct professor at East China Normal University in Shanghai. He is a PRC native with a PhD from Duke University in the USA. He writes extensively in both English and in Chinese. His case raises two interesting issues about the realities of contemporary Chinese intellectual life. First, despite his good scholarship, in recent years Professor Zhang has discovered that one of his important audiences has not been paying much attention to him. Despite the de facto essentialism of North American China studies which accords Zhang Xudong authority to speak on behalf of PRC intellectuals and Chinese people in general, that was demonstrably not the view of his PRC colleagues. PRC academics, such as Professor Liu Dong, have dismissed him as 'a foreign scholar' because he can live and work free of the constraints that face scholars working inside China. Indeed, one major reason why Zhang Xudong took an adjunct professorship at a major Chinese university was in order to be taken seriously by his Chinese peers again.

Second, with scholars like Zhang Xudong holding jobs throughout Western universities now, who is the Western scholar and who the Chinese 'subject'? On almost every topic covered in this book, from political science to literary studies to historical research, there are PRC natives trained in Western graduate schools who have published books in English. Yet their voice is not uniform. Some embrace postmodern approaches associated with Foucault or Derrida (such as Zhang Xudong), while others maintain formal Western social science models (such as Tong Yanqi) or attempt to blend them (as do Zhao Yuezhi and Zhao Suisheng).[33] While their childhood experiences in China and recent adventures as immigrants and visible minorities in Western societies surely shape their thinking, nonetheless their social experience as academics in the USA, Canada, and Europe increasingly defines their outlook. At the same time, however, globalizing forces of professionalism bring many of the same forces (tenure reviews, peer review academic publishing) to bear on academics like Liu Dong and Xu Jilin inside China.

The issues and ideas that engage these Chinese Establishment intellectuals show how the response to similar problems of sustainability or social justice differs in China compared to other societies. A key difference is the preferred mechanism for solutions. Democracy is not a widely embraced solution – at least, electoral democracy of the Western sort is not embraced by middle-class intellectuals 'for the time being.' A civil engineer, a woman who has been appointed to the National People's Congress, recently quoted Premier Zhou Enlai from the early 1950s:

> China is the most populous country on earth, and at present
> holding direct elections would be extremely difficult. As for equal

representation, peasants would make up 80 percent of the population, and so the majority of the deputies would also be peasants,
and that would not be any good.

'Now, a half a century on,' says the engineer NPC delegate, 'it still
holds true.' She goes on to say that she supports elections, and
even cites Lenin chapter and verse: 'Only universal, direct, fair
elections can be said to be democratic elections.' Her conclusion
suggests that democracy is good, but only among the right sort of
– educated – people.[34] Indeed, Wenfang Tang's survey data confirm
that even among non-Party or non-Establishment intellectuals there
is an acceptance that the most practical way to bring about concrete
political improvement is to work with the CCP.[35]

Three Chinas

These worlds of social and economic classes, and the intellectuals, cut across the face of China in a way that has created at least
three distinct societies within the PRC. Richard Madsen argues that
Chinese society today is 'a weakly united whole bound together
through codependent relationships' that make for a precarious
equilibrium.[36] Following the suggestion of Chalmers Johnson that
China should be thought of as three incompatible social systems
inside one country, Madsen goes on to give an articulate sociological
analysis of these three systems, identifying their distinctive internal
stratification system, pattern of life course, and cultural understandings of the proper relationship between self and society. His point
is that what it takes to make life work in, say, Third World China
contradicts what one needs to do in Newly Industrializing China,
yet the Chinese government and CCP as a single set of institutions
in a one-party state has to govern these three 'institutionally and
culturally incompatible social systems.' It is no easy task. These are
the three importantly different *social worlds* produced by reform.

Third World China In Third World China social status is heavily
dependent on one's position within families and corporate lineages.
Power, while needing Party and state approval, in practice depends
on informal and personal ties built around family and kin that
make local leaders into 'local emperors' who are very difficult for

the central authorities to control. A *successful life course* 'begins and ends with dependence on a male-dominated family. A comfortable and honorable old age in particular depends on being taken care of by one's adult sons and their wives. This system is *justified* by cultural values stressing the centrality of family, the importance of maintaining an orderly hierarchy of family authority, and the mutual obligations of family members.'[37] While not simply traditional, this system echoes long-standing cultural practices in rural China that have, ironically, been strengthened by the *hukou* system and communes under Mao, which locked the peasants on the land. Even in 2006, some 70 percent of Chinese – about 800 million people – live and make their permanent homes in this rural system.

Socialist China This is the world of the industrial and professional urban 'work units' (*danwei*) built under the State Plan in Mao's time, and it exists in all Chinese cities but is predominant in the old industrial northeast or Manchuria. In this social system, '*social status* has been dependent on rank within the bureaucratic hierarchies. *Power* is acquired by being sponsored by superiors within the Communist Party. A *satisfactory life course* depends on joining a satisfactory "work unit," moving up its bureaucratic ranks, and finally retiring on a pension provided by the work unit. The system is *justified* by what Andrew Walder has called "neo-traditionalism," a system of organized dependency under political paternalism.'[38]

Newly Industrializing China This, says Madsen, drives China's current economic dynamism through its 'market-driven, export-oriented manufacturing system.' In Newly Industrializing China '*status* is based on money (and displayed through conspicuous consumption). *Power* depends on personal connections with bureaucrats (bought with money), but not on adherence to bureaucratic rules. A *successful life course* depends on getting enough money to take care of oneself. All of this is *justified* by a social Darwinist ideology of progress through competition.'[39]

The value of Madsen's careful sociology of these three Chinas is that it clarifies how Chinese political economy operates today and

highlights the fragile, or what he calls the dysfunctional codependent, nature of the connections between the three systems. The capital
for China's dynamic export sector comes from the assets of the
socialist system as the state-owned industries are allowed to go
bankrupt and are stripped. The labor comes from Third World China
in the form of 150 million migrant laborers from the countryside.
What makes this system fragile is the wildly incompatible forms of
social life that the individuals who bring the capital and labor across
these social horizons must cope with, because it is individuals and
not rational systems which link these three worlds – government
officials turned entrepreneurs, rural laborers trying their luck in the
city, and urban families splitting jobs between the government and
market sectors. These people not only have no reliable rules to guide
them or legal recourse to protect them, but they must also 'translate'
between the patriarchal familial values of the countryside, the Party
norms of the old urban districts, and the rugged individualism of
new urban China. The pressure that threatens to blow all this up
is the suffering of the poor and anxieties of the middle class. As
Madsen concludes: 'China today is thus an unstable condominium
of at least three different social systems. For now, what ties them
together is codependency without synergy – a situation in which
it is in the interest of the most powerful people in each system to
maintain a status quo that exploits the weakest people within each
system.'[40]

Two worlds: human society and natural environment

Madsen has drawn a vivid picture of the dysfunctional family that
constitutes society in China today in his depiction of the three social
systems. To that we have to add material concerns: environment and
energy. If China is characterized by three distinct yet problematically
related social systems, then it is more precariously defined by two
worlds: the social and the natural. There is no pristine nature in
China, an area inhabited and exploited by human groups for some
five thousand years. Nonetheless, China today is on the brink of
crisis in its relationship to the land, water and air, which as Vaclav
Smil has warned for decades, goes well beyond smelly air and stinky
water; it threatens the ability of China to feed its people.[41]

The fabulous growth in Newly Industrializing China, plus continued inefficiencies in uses of energy in Socialist and Third World China, have made China energy hungry. There is a real danger that there will not be enough rice or light in the years ahead. The costs to China of these environmental problems are staggering – some 8–12 percent of GDP *annually*.[42] The list of environmental troubles is overwhelming. *Flooding*: not only on the Yangzi river in 1998 but also the Huai river (which demarcates the North and South China growing regions) in July 2001. On these and other rivers the flooding is caused by increased run-off from mountainsides denuded of trees upstream and fields covered with buildings and tarmac near by. *Desertification*: China's deserts are growing at an alarming rate, already 25 percent of the country, the rate of desertification has doubled in recent decades. Efforts to stem the spread of dust bowls through afforestation and grassland planting have had only limited success. *Water scarcity*: Skyrocketing demand, few conservation efforts, and massive pollution have limited access to potable water for 60 million people. Factories are closing and millions of people are having to leave their land, while water supplies for major northern cities from artesian wells are dangerously low. *Dwindling forest resources*: China has one of the lowest forest resources per capita in the world and most of that has been ruthlessly logged, often illegally, over the past three decades. In addition to the pending collapse of the forestry industry, loss of biodiversity, climate change, desertification, and soil erosion are all measurably on the rise. *Population growth*: Even Jiang Zemin, China's former General Secretary of the CCP, has called China's population size the biggest problem for the government. Population pressure drives much of China's resource degradation. While population growth is slowing, it is still a major issue.

It is this stunningly dynamic, unfair, and challenging system that the CCP tries to govern and in which Chinese of disparate social places try to get by. It is fair to ask: what would *any* government do? In fact, people in China do not simply try to survive, they respond, and it is the social responses to reform – efforts of winners to consolidate their gains, as well as the resistance of the losers – which have shaped Party policy and the continuing realities of living with reform in the recent decade.

5 | Winners and losers: reactions to reform

History is not on the minds of most people in China today; how to respond to their rapidly changing world is. Profiting from the new opportunities brought on by the reforms, or at least coping with their effects, dominates the daily life experience of men and women across China today. The lessons and challenges of the Mao years and the first decades of reform are very much on the minds of the CCP leadership in Beijing. But for these leaders, as well as ordinary people, the dynamics of contemporary Chinese domestic politics in the last five years are defined by the *reactions* to the consequences (intended and unintended) of reform.

The experience of reform, as we saw in Chapter 4, is not at all uniform across China or within a single community. To a large degree reactions to the consequences of reform are simple: as those of either winners or losers. These are not just passive experiences. People of like condition mobilize, respond, wheedle, complain, conspire, and sometimes hit the streets and stone the local government office. The Public Security Bureau acknowledged an astounding 86,000 public disturbances in China for 2005.[1] Internationally, China may be a stable and economically dynamic nation, but internally it is racked by contradictions that rightly alarm informed observers (whether in Beijing or London), worry the current social winners following reform and outrage the losers. It is the dynamics of these pervasive social contradictions which define life in China today – expressed in a cycle of government reforms, results both anticipated and unanticipated, reactions to reforms across society and parts of the state, and, finally, new policies. These reactions to reform will determine the future course of China as a state and international actor, as well as a society.

We can look at this cycle of reactions to reform and the struggle between winners and losers in terms of three contradictions: class conflict, competition between local and central governments, and the contradictions between growth and sustainability. There is a simmering class conflict brewing between the prosperous middle class along with the minuscule super-elite and the rural poor, laid-off industrial workers, and the lumpenproletariat of the 'floating population' of urban day laborers. These social conflicts have been acknowledged by the CCP leadership, through their solution – the harmonious society (*hexie shehui*).[2] But the Party's vaunted goals for the harmonious society have yet to be put into practice beyond a few token prosecutions of local bad guys and a sputtering campaign of repression against anti-state agitators, real or imagined.[3] The second contradiction is the undeniable emergence of *two states* in the one-party state: the central government and the local government. This reality is captured in the language of people in each locality. They speak of the *zhengfu*, the local state, which is usually the cause of their problems, and they speak of the *guojia*, the national government, which is usually their hope for redress of these problems. China may not be a multiparty system, but it is emphatically a bifurcated state system. For not only do local people perceive a meaningful difference between their local *zhengfu* and the distant *guojia*, but also the political elite itself is all too aware of this disjunction between central and local administrations. Beijing leaders bemoan the insubordination of local authorities, and local leaders know full well that (contrary to Western views about communist systems) the Leninist Party-State is in fact not strong enough to control all of them. The third key contradiction is between *growth and sustainability*, particularly resource and environmental sustainability. None of the actors in Chinese society, from the top leadership to the poorest farmer or day laborer, can continue to use the land, water, and air in the same ways and expect other than disaster in just a few decades. While social contradictions between rich and poor and central and local governments are more acute, it is the chronic contradiction of sustainability which will most fundamentally determine China's future. Only belatedly has the government leadership done more than talk the talk of conservation and sustainability, and only recently have social groups been able to mobilize to protest against the local destruction caused by industrial pollution.

These fundamental reactions to reform in contemporary China – class conflict, competition between central and local governments, and the challenge of sustainability – are muted in Western media coverage of China. To read major Western press reports one would think that life in China is dominated by the struggle with Falun-gong practitioners, fights with democratic dissidents, repression of Tibetan separatists, a massive arms build-up, and a burgeoning life on the Internet. Of these Western preoccupations, only the astonishing growth of the Chinese Internet among urban and middle-class Chinese accurately characterizes reactions to reform over the past decade. In the last section of this chapter we will look in more detail at the Chinese Internet and its major role in the expression of Chinese nationalism. There is much sound and sensitive reporting on China by serious journalists and thoughtful reflections on environmental, labor, and gender issues in China in Western news-papers and journals. These reports are not so much wrong (indeed, I have relied on several as indicated in the notes to this book) as misconstrued – the problems they raise about China are seen in *our* context, in terms of the concerns of citizens in Western societies. These reports are alienated from the social experience of various peoples and groups inside China. The goal of this chapter, as for this entire book, is to bring a more palpable sense of the social worlds and daily concerns of people across China and to remind us of the organizations and ideas they have to hand to deal not only with Tibet, Taiwan, or Falungong but also with the issues that confront us all – social justice in our community, environmental sustainability in our neighborhood, and regional security.

Social reactions to reform: consolidation, resistance, and conflict

Individual experiences of reform, naturally, vary even within social groups and levels of privilege. Individual experiences coalesce into social reactions, however, as consciously or unconsciously individu-als cooperate to pursue the interests that their social experience suggests to them. In China today, the winners seek to consolidate

the gains of reform. As we have seen, the CCP-dominated government seeks to create their version of a harmonious society that will
stabilize the current privileges of the Party elite. Similarly, the tiny
but fearsomely wealthy super-elite, along with the much broader
middle class, finds a confluence of interest with the Party elite in
pursuing this consolidation. Of these two levels of elites, the middle
class threatens the most portentous changes for China – as their
intellectuals pursue political liberalization in order to articulate middle-class interests and the material desires of the middle class drive
China's hunger for oil and other energy resources that it cannot,
according to most analyses, sustain. The middle class thus drives
both political democratization and environmental disaster. This dual
role of the middle class can be seen in the contrast between the
obvious environmental strains that their new consumption patterns
generate – to support millions of cars, electricity for appliances and
air conditioners, and materials for more spacious housing – and
their increasing role in China's emerging environmental movement.
The signature example of this is Friends of Nature, run since the
mid-1990s by the notable conservationist Liang Congjie. His Beijing-based environmental NGO is a classic example of the cautious
work-with-the-Party approach that has been favored by the middle
classes. Friends of Nature focuses on education, small grants to local
groups, and consultation on environmental reform.[4]

The losers are not without social resources. The industrial working
class in the state-owned factories constituted the touted 'leaders' of
socialist China under Mao. They know modern production methods
and how to organize. They are being laid off in huge numbers and
they are not happy about it. Some reorganize as individual entrepreneurs; others begin to agitate for compensation, and they are not
shy about using force, or, in the case of workers in Sichuan, taking
hostages. By 1997 the state-run Jianlihua silk factory, which used to
employ some 10,000 workers in Nanchong, Sichuan, had handed
out lay-offs and pay cuts for several years. Workers were angered by
the management's extravagances in such hard times. As the general
manager prepared for an official 'inspection tour' of Thailand with
his wife, the workers took him hostage:

> They loaded Huang [the manager] into the back of a flatbed
> truck and forced him into the painful and demeaning 'airplane
> position' – bent at the waist, arms straight out at the sides. Then
> they ... paraded him through the streets [of Nanchong] just like
> the Cultural Revolution. ... Workers from other factories joined the
> spontaneous demonstration ... 20,000 people took part.

After a stand-off of some thirty hours, the demonstration ended peacefully with the government ordering that back pay be given – via loans from the state-run bank.[5] Such violent demonstrations have become quite common, and it seems the Party is allowing them to occur, so long as they remain local, to punish local despots and to relieve the frustrations of strapped workers.

Farmers, the *nong* or peasants under Mao, similarly know how to run village and local elections, committees, and at times riots.[6] Depending on the level of misery and the contingencies of poor administration and available leadership in their own ranks, unhappy workers, farmers, homeowners, women's groups, or ethnic groups resist or outright fight back. Kevin J. O'Brien and Li Lianjiang have nicely captured the nuances of rural resistance as 'rightful resistance,' where farmers frame their claims in terms of the government's own promises and guarantees and where they join forces with officials inside the state administration who are willing to help. Intelligent efforts at rightful resistance far outnumber even the tens of thousands of public demonstrations across China. Together these are the forces that drive labor and environmental disputes, violent rural protests against corrupt local administrations, deal-making and compromises between local governments and communities, ethnic conflicts, increasing legal challenges, religious dissidence, and even muckraking journalism in China today. As we have seen, below these obvious social acts flow the very real and very influential subterranean currents of massive migration across China of people displaced by economic change or government takeover of fields and entire communities (particularly for dam construction) and the time-honored techniques of foot-dragging and non-compliance with government orders, from family planning rules to taxes to environmental standards.

Growth of counter-cultures from illegal Christian house churches to gay and lesbian communities exists not only in Shanghai, but also in rural communities.[7] China's diverse social experience quite naturally finds a diversity of social expression. The Chinese pluralism Susan Blum has noted for ethnic lifeways in China really extends throughout the warp and weft of the society, even the 'Three Chinas' of Third World China, Socialist China, and Newly Industrializing China.

Guojia and *zhengfu*: reform China's contending governments

The CCP's response to these social reactions to reform has been to talk about the 'harmonious society' and patriotism. The actions of the CCP, however, have focused on reasserting central fiscal and administrative control over China's wildly divergent and largely insubordinate local states. This is the struggle between the *guojia* (the central state) and the *zhengfu* (the local administration) that both local farmers and householders and Central Committee leaders recognize. The post-Mao reforms have devolved considerable financial and administrative control to the provinces and cities, counties and towns. Now the central government wants that control back, but the localities are loath to relinquish their new-found moneymaking powers. Much more so than battles with individual intellectual dissidents or democratic activists or even organized religious groups such as Falungong, the struggle between China's central government and local states is the most important political struggle in China today. The outcome of this fight will shape what can and cannot be done for women, workers, sustainability and, indeed, freedom of expression and association. It is not simply a battle between good guys and bad guys, but rather a fundamental renegotiation of the polity: who decides public policy and how.

Beijing's policy of the 'harmonious society' seeks to knit China's diversity together. This policy, put forward by President and Party leader Hu Jintao in 2004, is the CCP's response to the current cycle of reform and reaction. At heart, as we have suggested in earlier chapters, the CCP is now trying to shift from a focus on growth at any cost to a recognition of the need to address issues of equity. To enforce equity the center needs to be able to compel rich provinces to transfer some of their wealth to poorer areas or to forgo profitable business in order to give these opportunities to less-developed regions of China. While Westerners see the policy of the harmonious society as a cover for crackdowns on democratic dissidents (which is also true), China's regional leaders see it as an attempt by the center to put the bridle back on the localities. In all, Hu Jintao's approach can be called populist authoritarianism under which the CCP has found ways to strengthen its governing capacity while avoiding democratization.[8]

At the top, the nature of central government politics shapes what can be done. The experience of reform at the top levels of the CCP has produced what Cheng Li describes as 'one party, two factions' or as Chinese bipartisanship.[9] Li's key point is worth keeping in mind: in a one-party state that does not allow alternative political organizations, divergent social interests will have to find expression inside that party, or else explode on the streets. He suggests that there are now two relatively stable and cooperative factions within the top CCP that balance each other in ways similar to the role of competitive parties in liberal democracies – albeit with key differences stemming from the lack of electoral recall. Retired President Jiang Zemin and his current chief protégé, Zeng Qinghong (who is vice-premier of the PRC), head up a substantial faction that represents the interests of the elites in Chinese society, who have an interest in and commitment to policies that support *growth*. This faction is known as the Shanghai faction, because Jiang himself and many of his supporters in key positions in the central Party-State come from Shanghai. They speak for the Newly Industrializing China we saw in Chapter 4.

On the other hand, Hu Jintao, and his premier, Wen Jiabao, represent those leaders who served for many years in the inland provinces of Third World China (Hu in Tibet and Wen in Gansu). This faction is concerned with issues of *equity*, knowing full well the needs of the poorer regions and the capacity of the dispossessed for social unrest. They speak for Third World and Socialist (rust-belt) China. This faction is known as the Youth League faction, because so many of its leaders served in the CCP's Youth League – famously a home for reformist Party leaders since Hu Yaobang led the Youth League in the 1980s. Cheng Li's point is that these are not the same factions as we saw under Mao, which were built on the charisma of individual leaders or shared military experience in the revolutionary war, but rather are stable coalitions. More importantly these both represent meaningful social interests and also have in practice shared power. Today, very nearly half of the membership of key central Party and government committees can be identified with each of these two coalitions. While this is not a constitutionally protected form of political pluralism, it is a de facto bipartisanship that could, but not necessarily will, navigate the conflicting claims of growth and equity.

The CCP's populist authoritarianism under Hu Jintao has seen several efforts to strengthen the governing capacity of the central Party-State. New political institutions have been put in place. New social groups, particularly the new capitalists, have been incorporated into the Party. The Party has responded directly to popular protests, paying off debts where necessary and repressing nascent organizations that seem threatening. Finally, the Party has tried to win over the popular mind with this populist orientation. New political institutions to channel political participation and make a bridge between state and society include village elections, business and trade associations, and letters and visits to government offices. While there are real limitations to each of these initiatives, they reflect a broader effort undertaken by the CCP at administrative reform.

There have been remarkable efforts to improve administration at the municipal level. Kenneth Foster documents the case of Yantai, in Shandong, which implemented a Service Promise System among the city's bureaucracies, in a fashion explicitly drawing from the New Public Management model in Britain. These efforts included user-friendly websites and improved customer relations at city services – quite a shock for residents used to the surly bureaucrats of local China. While the publicity of the mid-1990s around the Yantai model, which was picked up by Beijing, has passed, there continue to be efforts, at least in the more prosperous areas of Newly Industrializing China, to promote this service-oriented public administration.[10] Huairou County, in the northern rural corner of Beijing's large administrative district, has a new five-story glass-and-steel administration building. The ground floor is given over to a large and welcoming public service center that would do any city in Canada or Britain proud. Cheerful and computer-equipped staff sit behind low and unintimidating counters, each with clear placards describing what official business can be conducted there. If one is confused, there are touch-screen computers just inside the front doors that guide citizens to the proper counter to handle their needs. Most astonishingly, at each counter the computer screens used by the staff are angled so ordinary citizens can see what is going on. On an ordinary day, one sees small clusters of locals leaning over one of the fifty or so counters in this long hall, in conversation with the staff and together looking at the computer screens. Similar scenes can be seen in the prosperous regions of Newly Industrializing China, from the suburbs of Guangzhou to the fast-growing Yangzi Delta region around Shanghai. This is the welcome side of China's administrative reforms, more transparent and efficient local government.

Indeed, the administrative reforms under Jiang Zemin and Hu Jin-tao have been extensive. It is as well to remember that the reluctance of the top CCP to democratize politics has not meant an inability to address fundamental issues of governance and state capacity. The key response of the CCP to the consequences of reform in the 1990s has been to strengthen the ability of the central state to discipline the provinces and localities and to develop capacity at all levels to regulate the economy. According to Dali Yang, 'China has made real progress toward making the Chinese state into a regulatory state suited to a functioning market economy.' Indeed, since Zhu Rongji's administrative reform plan was put forward in 1998, the PRC state has trimmed the size of the state administration, regularized the relationship between state institutions and business (as in getting the PLA out of the hotel business, for example), and strengthened the fiscal and regulatory powers of the state. It has also increased the number of People's Armed Police to 1 million.[11] Democracy is not on the CCP's agenda, but order and effective markets are.

At the same time, the CPP has sought to incorporate the new social groups that have arisen from reform. Key among these have been the new capitalists, or in Party terminology, entrepreneurs. Jiang Zemin famously invited capitalists to join the CCP in a 2002 speech and this was confirmed in the revised Party constitution of

2004. It is a sane choice for the Party if it wants to have business interests work with the Party-State. It is also an easy choice, because it is clear that business leaders in China would rather work with the State than attempt to articulate their interests in a separate political party.[12] Given that the Party has strengthened its ability to enforce central-level and macro-economic policy, this could contribute to a moderation of questionable business practices, such as over-investment in real estate, and a curbing of corruption. On the other hand, there is little reason to believe that the CCP's new entrepreneurial members will resist the opportunity to use state power to protect and extend their class interests.

The Party has also made a considerable effort to engage and incorporate intellectuals. While we have seen in Chapter 4 that many elite intellectuals and academics feel marginalized in the politically secular and increasingly commercial society of China today, many thousands have taken up the Party's invitation to contribute to its reform efforts directly as staff in its bureaucracy, researchers in its think tanks and Academies of Sciences and Academies of Social Science (which are operated under the CCP's propaganda system at each level of administration – central, provincial, and local). Additionally, intellectuals have availed themselves of the commercial opportunities of reform China – these allow a limited amount of public commentary and even muckraking journalism (but never involving high leaders), but in the main tend toward infotainment.[13] The limits to Party tolerance of intellectuals were shown in 2004 when the media publicity over the selection of 'China's 50 Public Intellectuals' in a Guangdong popular magazine, *People Weekly*, prompted Party criticism that the term 'isolated intellectuals from the People and the Party.'[14] Clearly, the Party's offer to work with intellectuals comes with the proviso: or else, stay out of the way.

As we have seen, the CCP has responded materially to the thousands of labor and rural protests against the abuses of local factories or local officials. The Party's response has been one of carrots and sticks. So long as the disturbances are local and issue-oriented, the Party will often pay the back wages, reinstate the pensions, provide compensation for land taken for development projects. As soon as such actions appear to be translocal or cross-class, however (most fearsomely, any signs of intellectual–worker/peasant coordination, such as appeared in Tiananmen in May 1989), the Party responds with repressive violence – arrests, police attacks, judicial cases, and long prison sentences.

This explains the treatment of the Falungong sect, which was banned by the Chinese government in 1999. In the 1990s Falungong was but one of a wave of popular religious and mystical sects that re-emerged across China. Falungong was unusual for two reasons. First, it was more religious in nature than many sport-oriented qigong groups. *Falun* means 'wheel of the [Buddha's] law' and *gong* means 'physical practice,' as in exercise or meditation. Falungong began by focusing on qigong exercises and was at the start a member of the state-sponsored qigong association (which included sports clubs involved with t'ai chi and other martial arts). But Falungong's Master, Li Hongzhi, had more religious aspirations. This brought about the group's second key significance: organization. Li Hongzhi withdrew his Falungong from the official qigong association, over finances or for some other unknown reason. This triggered official concern and the group began to suffer the depredations of an anxious state – surveillance, articles criticizing the group in the official press, permits to organize denied. Tensions between local Falungong groups and local governments flared, and in April 1999 Li Hongzhi organized a surprise peaceful 'sit-in' of several thousand adherents outside the gates of the CCP's leadership compound in Beijing, Zhongnanhai. This not only infuriated the top leadership, who were embarrassed and inconvenienced, but set off alarm bells in the halls of Leninist power – how could Falungong organize such a huge demonstration without the public security apparatus finding out in advance? The organizational capacities of Falungong were intolerable to the Chinese leadership and the sect was declared 'an evil cult' and banned in the summer of 1999. The persecution of Falungong members since then has been harsh and has rightly drawn world criticism.[15] The key point about the CCP's repression of Falungong is that the problem was not ideological – it had been legal for years as a wonky exercise cult – but organizational: thou shalt not have any other Party but My Party.

In all, the Hu–Wen administration has taken on a populist

orientation to back up their authoritarian rule. Their claim to 'feel the pain' of the poor (as former US President Bill Clinton was wont to say) may or may not be taken at face value by various Chinese, but it is clear that Hu and Wen have set a policy challenge for their government. The parallels to Peronism in Latin America are, of course, suggestive. Peronism – the economic, political, and social ideology called *Justicialismo* (social justice) – is associated with the rule of Juan Domingo Perón in Argentina in the mid-twentieth century. The CCP's current policy of 'harmonious society' offers a similar combination of nationalism and social democracy under an authoritarian regime, though there is hardly the devotion to the leader in China today to parallel the real popularity of Perón, other than through the memory of Mao. As Steven Levitsky has argued for the Latin American case, however, this Chinese Peronism is proving remarkably effective at transforming itself from a party of the workers to the party of neoliberal reform.[16]

China and the natural world

While the contradictions between China's revived social classes and between the central and local states dominate our story, it is the relationship between China and the natural world which will determine the sustainability not only of the current CCP regime but of Chinese society in all aspects. This is the third key contradiction in the responses to reform in China today. Social and political problems are urgent and are the scenes of immediate human suffering, resistance, and conflict, but problems of sustainability are important. Our story, so far, has noted the terrible costs in terms of air and water pollution, desertification and resultant flooding, the precipitous sinking of the water table and the loss of cropland that have come about as a consequence of China's reform and economic rise over the past three decades. This list of indicators is long and getting longer: nearly 80 percent of China's infamous city smog is caused by burning low-grade fuel. Who will pay the cost for better fuel? In the 1990s the World Bank judged that six of the ten most polluted cities in the world are in China. Throughout the first decade of the twenty-first century North China has had annual droughts and South China annual floods – all attributable to deforestation, erosion, and inappropriate dam construction. In 2003 droughts affected 60 million hectares and led to crop failure on 7 percent of all arable land in China. Beijing uses over 200 percent of its annual renewable ground water supply and the water table in North China around Beijing is falling at the rate of 3 meters a year.[17]

The reaction to these environmental problems has only just begun to be seen. The government talks a good line – setting up a State Environmental Protection Administration (SEPA) that works with Environmental Protection Units in major ministries and Environment Protection Bureaux in local governments.[18] Although SEPA was promoted to ministry status in 1998, it still does not have the teeth to enforce environmental protection policies over the interests of major ministries such as Construction, Defense, or Electricity. Despite an impressive number of White Papers on the environment, there is precious little implementation. But there likely will be more in the near future, and the reason is the Olympics. Beijing will host the 2008 summer Olympics and preparations are everywhere to be seen – lavish construction, cheerful logos, and constant discussion of social as well as material preparations for the world event in the local media. Air pollution in Beijing in 2006 is absolutely shocking, however. Months go by with only a few days of 'blue sky' – the foul haze (a mix of car exhaust, cement dust from hundreds of building sites, and industrial pollution) that shrouds buildings a few hundred meters away in fog continues day after day. The short-term solution in 2008 will, no doubt, be to turn the factories off and ban the cars. Already, new building permits in Beijing are not available – so the construction dust will settle over the next two years. The long-term solutions are not so easy and it is not at all clear that the government has the willpower to pay for changes to cars, factories, and transportation to end this smog on a sustainable basis.

Chinese citizen groups are beginning to mobilize. We have seen, above, the case of the Friends of Nature, the Beijing-based environmental NGO that seeks to work with the government on modest programs of environmental protection. At the central level, organization of environmental groups is lively, but not a simple case of 'civil society' sprouting in Chinese soil. The whole idea of an NGO, says Jonathan Schwartz, is complicated in China's political scene. There are at least three distinct kinds of environmental NGOs that have sprung up in China since 1994: traditional (Western-style, independent) NGOs, GONGOs (government-organized NGOs), and semi-NGOs. Traditional NGOs, such as Friends of Nature, have limited impact because they lack resources (there being little tradition of private philanthropy after decades of state socialism) and they must carefully avoid any organizational success that would make the government look at them as a new Falungong threat by registering with the Ministry of Civil Affairs. GONGOs, such as the China Environmental Protection Foundation, live as adjuncts to an official ministry, in this case on the web page of SEPA. They do good things, such as extra environmental awareness training for key leaders, but they are utterly subject to government control. Finally, a new form of response to environmental problems is the semi-NGO: environmental NGOs attached to major universities. They do not have to register with Civil Affairs, nor are they subject to SEPA. The Beijing Environment and Development Institute, housed at the People's University in Beijing, is one example. The goals of these semi-NGOs are, however, similar to those of the GONGOs: to train central government officials on environmental issues. The new contribution of the semi-NGOs is that they are freer to advocate for the dispossessed and to encourage and equip willing government officials to take on vested interests, such as ministries and big companies opposed to implementing environmental protection policies.[19]

Across China communities address environmental issues in their resistance and protests for the simple reason that the destruction of their farmland or the poisoning of their wells is what has brought them to the streets. The problem, as we have seen in earlier chapters, is that these local concerns are not connecting with similar concerns in the next county or province, or nationally. That is, they are not organizing. And they can't: the Party continues to watch carefully and to step on any signs of trans-local organization. The environmental NGOs we have discussed painstakingly avoid the appearance of such 'illegal organizing.' The likely path for articulating the interests of citizens of villages, counties, and towns where environmental disasters loom or have already crashed down upon their heads will probably have to be cooperation with local authorities. Despite the justified bad reputation of local government in China today, there are signs (at least in more prosperous regions such as Yantai and Beijing's Huairou county which we saw above) of responsible officials who want to make their home areas cleaner, safer, and more prosperous. The habit of Chinese intellectuals and NGOs to 'work with the government' has real promise for creating a new citizen–state alliance to address the problems of reform.

Commerce, of course, has responded to China's environmental crisis, as well – by trivializing environmental concerns through promoting 'green tourism.' An entire industry has grown up to get you out of the Beijing or Guangzhou haze for your holiday to 'quaint and colorful' minorities areas in Yunnan, Sichuan, and now by super-fast, pressurized express train to Lhasa. This environmental tourism not only does precious little to resolve the prime causes of pollution and resource degradation, but at the same time trades on Han chauvinist images of the Noble Savage in Yunnan or the yeoman farmer in Sichuan, as viewed from your air-conditioned bus spewing diesel fumes from its poorly tuned engine.[20] The market joins nationalism to form the twin distractions from China's challenges.

Nationalism and the Internet

The content of Hu Jintao's new populist orientation, however, is not all new in Chinese political culture and not at all subject to popular cynicism. There is another part of the Party line that is indisputably popular and provides an integrative force in China today – nationalism. Hu Jintao's recitation of the goals of the harmonious society includes the hegemonic story of China's historical humiliation and resurgence, which has brought the CCP real popular legitimacy since Mao's 1940 desiderata, 'On New Democracy' (see Chapter 1). In 2005, Hu Jintao explained to the Fortune 500 Forum in Beijing what they needed to know about 'China and the New Asian Century':

> Beginning in the mid-19th Century, China was reduced to dire misery as the country suffered one humiliating defeat after another and the people languished in poverty and starvation as a result of brutal foreign aggression and corrupt and incompetent feudal rulers.

Refusing to submit to a fate of agony and woe, the Chinese people fought back and finally built up a New China under the leadership of the Chinese Communist party.[21]

It is the nationalistic aspirations of the CCP's populist authoritarianism which have most effectively tapped into popular interests and sentiments. But it is a dangerous game: casting the CCP as the defender of national pride gives the Party widespread legitimacy; as we shall see, however, popular nationalism in China is very volatile and has already pushed the Party toward confrontational policies that have endangered not only China's chances of ultimate prosperity but also immediate regional security.

Given the powerfully diverse social experiences and regional diversity of China, as well as the considerable limitations in the will and state capacity of the CCP to address the centrifugal forces we have seen across the country, it is no surprise that China's leaders have latched on to the integrative powers of nationalism. This is not unique to China. America has succeeded in unifying a very diverse society around a set of ideas about the nation and the world – generally known as 'manifest destiny' – which suggest common purpose to its citizens in spite of centrifugal social realities.[22] The key point is that nationalism, both as a kind of shared pride in national achievement and as a projection of one's nation onto the global stage, has succeeded in both America and China in distracting public discussion from social disparities and other tensions that reside within their societies.

In the Chinese case, this integrative ideology has been a version of popular nationalism that Suisheng Zhao has identified as *qiang guo meng* – 'the dream to make China rich and strong.'[23] The key to such a successful integrative ideology is that it is both coherent enough to produce some unity of identity and loyalty to a center and is, at the same time, flexible enough to accommodate persuasive images of diverse experience.[24] The expression of this *qiang guo meng* nationalism today is 'China Rising' (*Zhongguo jueqi*). It has something for everyone, providing that integrative force and distraction from social tensions that nationalism delivers – but at the cost of ignoring underlying social and environmental time bombs. For the ruling elite

China Rising stands for success and redemption of China's rightful role as a world power. For the super-elite and middle classes it dignifies and justifies their search for (and achievement of) personal material wealth. For the working class it is the goal – they take pride in the public display of China's wealth and power from the gaudy Pearl Tower in Shanghai to China's notable space program. When they feel they can and are doing better, they discipline themselves to China's new market labor order. When they feel cheated, then the promises of China Rising are their justifications to resist or rebel. For China's underclasses it is a distant dream. China's media tell them that history is to blame and local norms blame the victim for being uneducated or for having 'bad fate' or for lacking the 'qualities' (*suzhi*) of modern citizens. While the poor suspect the agents of their immiseration are closer to hand in the form of local leaders and those very middle classes, they lack articulation and organization because they lack social capital or leadership and devote all their waking hours to survival.

China's Internet feeds this nationalism but also constantly threatens to turn the Party's clever distraction into pointed political dissent. Popular nationalism is the devil of diplomacy for China's leaders.[25] Online discussions and 'chat-rooms' dedicated to defending China's national dignity from US, Japanese, or other insults is a marvelous distraction from domestic policy failures but is a two-edged sword that threatens to lop off the heads of Chinese leaders after taking a swipe at foreign offenders. Throughout the twentieth century, Chinese states used popular resentment (usually, but not always, among the urban literate classes) at foreign imperialism to gain legitimacy and to bargain with foreign powers, but since the 1990s popular nationalism has frequently overwhelmed state plans, gone too far, and threatened international relations, and most ominously turned its fierce gaze from the wrongdoings of foreigners to the complicity of China's current leaders. To change metaphors, harnessing popular nationalism for diplomatic power and domestic relief is for China's leaders a case of 'riding the tiger' – effective, but it is not easy to get off the beast without it also eating you.

There are signs of democratic change on the Chinese Web. While the PRC has put up Internet firewalls to block international websites and e-mails dealing with sensitive subjects, from Tibet to Falungong, and China's intellectuals avoid direct confrontation with the state, liberal and democratic practices are emerging on the Chinese Web. The important changes come as much from the daily practice of ordinary users as from the extraordinary efforts of critics, as with the case of the Chinese edition of the user-developed online encyclopedia, Wikipedia.[26] The Chinese Internet is huge and growing. Some 111 million people are estimated to be online, with thousands joining every day. The Wikipedia website is not a hotbed of political commentary, it is a reference tool. Yet it is an open-authored site that requires the community of contributors to monitor themselves (this is the case for Wikipedia in every country). The Chinese-language site was launched in May 2001 and was heavy on science and technology. The first political debate among contributors came in July 2003 when a Hong Kong participant contributed an essay on 'China-centrism.' This led to differing views and a debate on how contributors should resolve their disputes. Some suggested privileging the views of the most active contributors, others advocated one user, one vote. But all, interestingly, accepted the goals of neutrality in the governing principles of Wikipedia – objectivity in content, equality among users, the importance of consensus.[27] The Internet serves China's dissidents, as well. Liu Xiaobo, the notable Chinese literary intellectual and scholar who returned from studies in the USA to participate in the 1989 Tiananmen demonstrations and who served time in Chinese jails, remains active in Beijing as a social and political critic. He recently posted an article, 'The Internet and Me,' in which he describes how e-mail and electronic file transfer make his organizing of petitions and publishing of articles possible.[28] While Liu cannot publish in China, he can work, write, and receive payment for publishing articles overseas. Clearly, the authorities know what Liu is doing, but they seem content to let him, so long as he does not stir up 'disturbance' inside China.

Nationalism is not the only integrating force in Chinese society. There are others, such as the hierarchical and patriarchal familialism that, for example, focuses on the male child, whether in a poor village or the family of a university professor. But the nationalism of China Rising not only helps us understand one very important shared ideology that knits Chinese pluralism together, but also helps explain two social facts of China today: its prickly popular national-ism and the ruthlessness with which the state represses any hint of organization among the populace that might give voice to the discontents of the losers under reform. China Rising in China today is a social myth on the level of Manifest Destiny in the USA or the White Man's Burden in Victorian England. It serves as an emotion-ally charged metaphor for the hopes and aspirations of different social classes in China, even though the content of that metaphor is meaningfully different for a middle-class engineer or a migrant worker in Shanghai or for a wealthy entrepreneur or poor farmer in Guizhou. All these people are *furious* at the Japanese for their school history textbooks, which slight China's dignity. One need only think of the American farmer in Kansas in the 1980s with the bumper sticker 'Assahola Kockumeiny,' or US TV news anchor Tom Brokaw's conversation with Crips gang members in Los Angeles in 1989 who wanted to know what was going on in Tiananmen. Neither farmer nor gang member had other than metaphorical concerns about Iran or China, but they felt those concerns deeply because, as Richard Madsen has suggested, these foreign policy issues directly touched foundational identity myths of American society.[29] The foundational myth is not, in either the US or the Chinese case, a simple icon, however; rather it is a debate: the challenge of what is a shared vision of the good and the right and the ongoing debate over how to achieve that, be it America's promise of a second chance for all or China's Rising.

6 | China in the world today

China is fuzzy around the edges, both geopolitically and culturally. Is Taiwan Chinese? If Hong Kong is now part of the PRC, how come it is harder for Chinese citizens to visit this bit of southeast China than to visit Thailand or Europe? Is Tibet part of China? And what of the tens of millions of Chinese descendants spread across nearly every country of Southeast Asia, as well as 'Overseas Chinese' in Australia, Europe, and the Americas? China is embedded throughout the world. Conversely, the world is increasingly inside China. Why do so many people in urban China like McDonald's? What is Chinese about suburban homes, car commutes or white-dress wedding photos? The simple answers offered by our sensationalist free press and distracted politicians (as well as China's own sensationalist unfree press and worried politicians) is that China is a growing power with nationalistic leanings and is both an economic and military power to take seriously. 'China Rising' (*Zhongguo jueqi*) is the slogan that has taken hold, though it means good things to various Chinese and is a cause for grave concern to most Western leaders.

When it comes to talking about China in the world, the urge to talk in unitary terms of 'China does this' or 'China wants that' is nearly unavoidable. It has been the main task of this book, however, to inoculate us against such an easy mistake. Surely, the nation-state of the People's Republic of China matters and its policies – in global trade regimes, at the UN, or on the South China Sea – matter and its military might is real. But we know that China is more a continent than a country, that the internal diversity of China is staggering, and that the first concern of people in China from the street vendor to the middle-class car owner to the Beijing bureaucrat is domestic and not international. Yet those local and domestic concerns have been powerfully influenced by the forces of economic and cultural globalization, from the price of local crops to the availability of foreign TV shows. And in turn, those domestic concerns drive China's foreign policy, as is the case for most nations. In the end, however, when it comes to China's role in the world, it is as much a foolish distortion to paint all Americans with the brush of George W. Bush and his policies as it is to paint all people in China with the brush of Mao Zedong or the latest bit of propaganda coming out of Beijing.

In order to counter the tendency to abstract complex international relations into 'Beijing,' 'Washington' or, worse, 'the Americans' or 'the Chinese,' we will approach China in the world from the bottom up, from lived experience to public expressions of identity to state foreign policy. We begin with the 'ungrounded empires' of daily life for people in China and for people who identify with China across the world. We then look at the societies that make up the PRC's fragile peripheries, from Tibet to Taiwan. Finally, we look at China's Rising as a world power and an international player. In this way we should be able to see the diversity and tensions behind the simple headlines. More importantly, we should be able to see past the alarmist tales in the Western press and focus on the challenges and problems people in China share with people everywhere: social justice, environmental sustainability, and regional security.

Ungrounded empires

The world is now in urban China. As the anthropologist James L. Watson well described it in 2000:

> Looming over Beijing's choking, bumper-to-bumper traffic, every tenth building seems to sport a giant neon sign advertising American wares: Xerox, Mobil, Kinko's, Northwest Airlines, IBM... American food chains and beverages are everywhere in central Beijing: Coca-Cola, Starbucks, Kentucky Fried Chicken, Häagen-Dazs, ... and of course, McDonald's.[1]

To Watson's description we could add an equal list of European and other international products and outlets, and we can confirm that in the six years since his census these international brands have only increased, and spread to smaller cities. Starbucks can now be had in nearly every provincial capital of China, and Rolex and Northface jackets – or watches and jackets with those brand names emblazoned on them – can be bought at street markets in even county towns. Deng Xiaoping wanted China to open to the world, and the world has stepped right in. Yet lattes and Big Macs do not turn Beijing residents into Americans, and rural China – where 70 percent of the population still lives – sees little of these global brands and services that so delight the urban middle classes.

China is also in the world, and has been for over five hundred years. If we want to understand the experience of China in the world today from the ground up, it is best to begin with Chinese communities in Vancouver and Melbourne, San Francisco and Penang. These are parts of what Aihwa Ong and Donald Nonini call the 'ungrounded empires' of overseas Chinese. Tens of thousands of Chinese, mostly laborers and merchants, have lived and worked outside China for centuries and kept contact with their home towns in China. Sizable Chinese communities have been active in trade and labor in the 'South Seas' (*nanyang*) of Southeast Asia since the fourteenth century.[2] They have been active in the Americas, Australia, and Europe since at least the middle of the nineteenth century. These sojourning communities connected China on an everyday basis to other parts of the world in two important ways. First, these communities have been part of their host societies, though the relationships have been filled with racism, oppression, and struggle. Second, the members of these communities, by and large, stayed connected to their natal areas inside China proper, traveling back and forth and sending money home. By the twentieth century these far-flung communities and the business power of many of their merchants created the ungrounded empires of overseas Chinese.[3] This key aspect of China in the world has passed underneath the radar of nation-to-nation relations. Yet, as any historian of life in California, New South Wales, or Lyons knows: the presence of Chinese migrants since the nineteenth century has been an important part of US, Australian, or French history.

The name for these Chinese outside of China is a political construction. *Huaqiao* or Overseas Chinese is a term that was coined only in 1893 and adopted by the Chinese republican government in the early twentieth century to claim the authority to bargain on behalf of these communities of Chinese in the Americas and Europe, in particular.[4] The term assumes that individual Chinese living outside China are still political Chinese and will, ultimately, return. This political designation was not out of line with most personal intentions among these sojourners at the time. Most of these migrants were from poor regions in South China (Guangdong and Fujian provinces, north and south of Hong Kong, in particular) and traveled only under duress – to make money for their families and for themselves. Their intention was to work in Old Gold Mountain (San Francisco of the American Gold Rush in the 1840s), New Gold Mountain (Melbourne of the Australian Gold Rush of the 1850s), or Mexico, Southeast Asia or other places where work could be found or business opportunities beckoned. These connections worked through family, clan, and local organizations.

Over time these sojourners have connected China with the world through a web of a thousand individual strands. Beneath, around, and over the 'Great Wall' of Chinese political isolation in the twentieth century these human connections have continued to operate – going dormant during wars hot or cold, only to revive at the first sign of peace. These overseas Chinese have been used by all recent Chinese governments, from the Qing Dynasty in the late nineteenth century to Chiang Kai-shek's republican government to Mao's and the current CCP leadership, to help China survive and prosper. The role of Overseas Chinese in the larger process of 'China in the world' is, however, complex and varies by personal identity. A Canadian of Cantonese descent whose parents were born in Canada may hold a very different identity from, and, as far as China is concerned, play a hugely different role to, a first-generation, PRC-born, new Canadian. These Chinese (mostly of the Han ethnicity) have become permanent residents and citizens of dozens of nations around the globe. 'Overseas Chinese' now points not to the limited juridical conception of *huaqiao*; rather they, and the PRC government, now say *waiji huaren*, Chinese with foreign citizenship. Overseas Chinese now enjoy – or endure, depending on one's personal perspective – what Aihwa Ong calls 'flexible citizenship.'[5] Their faces make them visible minorities in the Americas (with large communities in Brazil and Mexico, as well as in the USA and Canada), in Australian and European societies, as well as recognizable immigrants in most other societies around the world, but literally millions of these sons and daughters of sojourners are now native-born Americans, Canadians, etc. This is one of the most significant ways that China is in the world today.

The history of these Chinese in the broader world has been troubled and important for both China and their new homes and suggests that their significance in the twenty-first century will continue. Two examples will suffice to indicate the profound importance of this lived experience for China. The first comes from the sixteenth century and is an example of China's connections to the world, to processes of globalization that both pre-date our idea of globalization as something new in the twentieth century and in ways that extend beyond conscious human experience. The connection is food, the sweet potato, as well as corn (maize). Both came from Spanish Mexico to the Philippines and thence to China as an unintended consequence of the very intentional trade in silver across the Pacific. Until the early nineteenth century, European trade with China was a case of a backwater wanting to get the goods of the center of world economic activity – particularly porcelain, teas, furniture, and silk products. The Europeans had nothing that Chinese consumers wanted (even the marvelous clocks that Jesuits flaunted to Chinese aristocrats garnered little more than mild curiosity). What the Europeans had that Chinese merchants did want was silver, or rather they had Mexican silver. So, silver from the mines of the Spanish New World empire went directly to Asia to pay for those imports. Along the way, sailors brought cheap food that would last on the long voyages, the American tuber, the sweet potato. This moved from the Spanish ports in the Philippines, where overseas Chinese merchants brought the goods for silver exchanges, to ports in China.

The net result was a catastrophic population boom in China in the eighteenth century. Chinese who had never met a Spaniard or an Amerindian, not to mention never benefited from the silver (other than to endure inflation), were profoundly affected by China's role in the early modern world economy. In brief, the sweet potato survives drought better than rice or other grains. Maize grows on dryer hillsides where rice either cannot or would require laborious terracing. Thus, the diffusion of these food staples allowed generations of farming Chinese both to survive and to continue to reproduce during recurrent droughts in various parts of China that had, in previous centuries, contributed to keeping China's total population in the realm of 100–150 million. By 1850 it had shot up to around 450 million.[6] This phenomenal population growth combined with a political system and ideology that did not embrace change contributed, but did not in itself cause, the decline of the Qing Dynasty. In 1712 the Kangxi Emperor declared 'No New Taxes,' and he meant it. While reflecting a noble Confucian political theory to keep government from oppressing the farmer, the fixed national income in the face of a doubling of population led to a marked decline in governing capacity and a rise in local official corruption. This is not to blame the fall of the Qing on the sweet potato, but rather to highlight the importance of China's long-term connections to and interactions with the global economy *for many centuries*. Globalization is not new, especially for China.

Hundreds of years later, we see the impact of Overseas Chinese for modern China in the context of the cold war. As the McCarthy period dominated US politics in the 1950s, American scientists of Chinese descent were subject to political persecution as 'likely' spies for communist China. Amont them was Qian Xuesen, a US citizen and scientist who worked on ballistic missiles. An officer in the US Army in World War II, Qian was a student of the great Von Kasmann at Caltech (who started the Jet Propulsion Lab). Qian worked in military aerospace during and after the war. In the 1950s, however, he was subjected to political investigation by US authorities, prohibited from continuing his professional work, and hounded by agents of the US government. In the end, despite his claims of loyal service to the USA, he was driven out. As a result of this repression, he rediscovered his Chinese identity, was warmly embraced by the new PRC, and 'returned home' to China (having originally moved to America in 1935), where he became the leader of the Chinese ballistic missile program and worked on the eventual successful development of the famous Chinese-made anti-ship missile, the Silkworm.[7] In this sense, the racism and fear-mongering that have plagued Chinese sojourner communities in the USA (and most other societies) since the nineteenth century contributed to the very thing that xenophobia feared: American military technology getting into the hands of communist competitors. As with the sweet potato, this one instance did not determine all. For example, the Soviet Union provided considerable military technology in the 1950s before pulling out in 1960 over intra-socialist disputes before the final development of a Chinese A-bomb. Qian's case shows, however, both the significance and ironies of the complex personal experiences of China in the world.

These intellectual and social connections between China and the wider world that have shaped China today also provide 'Chinese' alternatives available to those unhappy with the current CCP leadership. The most obvious example for socialist China is the role of the anarchist-organized work-study program to Europe for Chinese students in the 1910s. Deng Xiaoping and other future leaders of the CCP worked and studied in France and other European nations, seeing, in particular, the disasters the West inflicted upon itself in the Great War (World War I). By the 1920s Chinese students were studying in their thousands in both the USA and the USSR. In fact, of all Chinese students who studied overseas between 1890 and 1930, over 80 percent studied in nearby Japan. These students embraced a range of political ideologies and brought them home – anarchism, social Darwinism, Bolshevism, liberal democracy, Christianity. While the complex social and political realities and contingent events (such as the Japanese invasions of China between 1931 and 1945) produced a socialist China in 1949, these other ideologies did not disappear. Today, as Chinese intellectuals seek alternatives to the dystopian version of Maoism that characterized the 1970s they cast back to their own earlier international history – a history of Chinese liberalism as put forth by Hu Shi and James Yen, of the revived Confucianism of Liang Shu-ming, of a less statist socialism of Qu Qiubai. The major political ideologies of the twentieth century circulate in China today not purely under foreign monikers, but in terms of the names, lives, and works of hundreds of Chinese who engaged with these ideas in the first half of the twentieth century.[8] There has been a wholesale 'rediscovery' of republican China (1911–49) among PRC academics and in China's intellectual journals. When Chinese public intellectuals promote liberalism or social democracy, they have to hand dozens of Chinese examples from this international history of Chinese social activism.

This international history goes in the other direction, from China to the world, as well. Today, Chinese communities across the planet form a part of what Harvard sinologist Tu Wei-ming calls 'Cultural China' (*Wenhua Zhongguo*).[9] Professor Tu has in mind intellectuals – both Chinese who have made their way in the universities of Western societies and non-Chinese who have become expert in Chinese language and culture. Indeed, this diaspora of middle-class and educated Chinese has created a social base for the revival of Confucianism. Tu Wei-ming calls this the Third Epoch of the teachings of Confucius – the first being the original ancient philosophy around the time of the Roman Empire and the second being the neo-Confucianism that evolved in the eleventh century CE as a Chinese response to and partial integration with the challenge of Buddhism. Seen in this *longue dureé*, a Taiwanese Chinese working at Harvard (Tu Wei-ming) or an Anglo-American scholar of ancient Chinese, Henry Rosemont, Jr, is not such a strange member of a Chinese family broadly construed.[10]

Cultural China is far broader and much of it much more vulgar than the émigré Confucianism espoused by Tu Wei-ming. Hong Kong has driven the international culture of China for many decades via the humble entertainment products of the marketplace: kung fu fighting films and Cantopop music.[11] This pop-rock fusion with classical Chinese poetry for lyrics or edgy material from J-pop (yes, Japanese pop) not only provides the common mass entertainment culture for Hong Kong, and inspiration to rockers in the PRC, but is part of a growing eastern Asian popular culture market that in the mid-2000s is now dominated by Korean singers and actors. It is a huge market engaging tens of millions of teens and young adults from Tokyo to Kunming and Hong Kong to Harbin. For China, Cantopop (known as *Gang-Tai* music, from Xiang*gang*, the Mandarin pronunciation of the characters for Hong Kong, and *Tai*wan) came to the fore in none other than the famous 1989 student protests in Tiananmen Square. There, the Taiwanese pop singer Hou Dejian became a musical signature of the protests (that he visited the square during the demonstrations in May was, at the very least, cunning marketing). The music scene in the PRC has matured and now there is Mandopop – Mandarin pop music (in Mandarin Chinese instead of the Cantonese dialect of Hong Kong). It is so utterly ordinary to young, urban Chinese today that this pop music does not strike them as particularly or meaningfully foreign.[12] As James Watson noted about McDonald's in the decade or more since the first one opened in Beijing in 1993, young Chinese assume that these pieces of urban culture are local, and in any event are authentically their own.

Beyond these outstanding examples, it is well to remember the ordinary life of Chinese overseas communities. They are defined by family, minority identity, and continuing linkages to natal communities in China. Some try to fit in with their new homes, taking Thai surnames, American citizenship, or Dutch marriage partners. These are the people we see in our communities, each to a greater or lesser extent connected to these ungrounded empires. Some embrace a dual identity, or flexible citizenship, seeing no necessary contradiction in service to two communities – their current home of citizenship and their ancestral and cultural home in China. Others feel no connection. Youth of Chinese descent in the West often share the guilt – and the Saturday language schools – with those of Jewish descent and their complex relationship with Israel. Western universities are full of 'heritage students' with Chinese faces who now want, or feel obliged, to learn the Chinese language and 'find their roots.' Whatever the person's experience, the linkages back to China are most usually family or locality, and in any case personal rather than official.

What these enduring connections of ungrounded empires and cultural China mean for residents across China is varied. The different roles these international connections play are mediated by the complex array of social and regional 'places' inside China. For middle-class academics in Shanghai and Beijing, social democracy and the ideas of Vaclav Havel or Jurgen Habermas are food for thought. The intellectual impact of China in the world, however, is not limited to urban or middle-class China. Thus, an American-trained native of a Shaanxi village now teaches as a professor in Macao, publishes in English scholarly journals, as well as Chinese-language media, works on China–Taiwan relations, but goes back regularly to his relatively poor village to help in development efforts. He is not planning to give up his international academic career, but he will clearly be a force in a part of northwest China that we have characterized as 'Third World China.' Families from the four counties around Guangzhou (Canton) have long played similar roles, though more often in terms of sending remittances, building large family homes, lineage temples, and improved graves for ancestors, and by investing in township-village enterprise (TVE) and other industry.

Today we see the impact of the Internet for these ungrounded empires and the two-way interaction between them and residents inside the PRC. This technology is backed up by the social experience of talented intellectuals and professionals. As we saw in Chapter 5, whether living and working outside China or inside, many use the Chinese-language websites (which will soon form the majority of websites and the major language of the Web) to address issues of concern inside China. This is a new ungrounded empire of the Web.[13]

The largest impact of overseas Chinese inside China comes from those nearest and uses personal visits and business investments rather than Internet connections. These are the *tongbao* – compatriots of Hong Kong and Taiwan. Since the 1980s the largest single source of investment and the greatest number of joint venture enterprises in reform China have come from, and been managed by, entrepreneurs from Hong Kong and Taiwan. These have sometimes been built on family lines or personal connections, but by and large these investments have been primarily business. As we have seen in previous chapters, it has, regrettably, often been a fairly sordid business involving bribes, sweatshop labor, pollution, and corruption. The low status of farmers and migrant workers contributes to the labor abuses in these Hong Kong and Taiwanese factories in China.

China's fragile peripheries

The lived experience of residents of China with communities outside the PRC is not, however, limited to Han Chinese or to Chinese identity. This leads us to China's fragile peripheries around the PRC – Taiwan, Korea, Southeast Asian states, the new states of

Central Asia, Mongolia, and Russia – as well as the troubled communities inside the PRC that in many ways have more in common with their neighbors than with Beijing – Tibet, Xinjiang, and even Hong Kong.

China's fragile peripheries are a central problem for China in the world today.[14] First, the border communities are minority populations that, as we saw in Chapter 1, occupy about a quarter of the PRC's total territory and sit atop riches of oil and natural gas. China needs these resources and needs peace to tap them efficiently. But relations between Tibetans or Uighurs and the majority Han population are not good, and Beijing's solution is controversial – virtual ethnic drowning by importing hundreds of thousands of Han into Tibet and Xinjiang. Second, these areas border China's neighbors. Unrest in those countries can easily bleed into China. Beijing remains deeply worried about 'international terrorism' (national liberation movements), especially among Central Asian Muslims, such as the Uighurs in Xinjiang. Third, the fragile accommodations on the edges of the PRC include two key Han populations – those in Hong Kong and Taiwan. Hong Kong is back in the PRC as of 1997 but is turning out to be something of a democratic thorn in the side of Beijing. Taiwan remains infuriatingly outside the CCP's grasp. The leadership is torn between 'getting Taiwan back' by talk or by force. Meanwhile, most politicians in Taiwan scoff at any talk of 'getting back' to China – they feel they have been an independent society for over a century. They might join the PRC, since they share culture and heritage, but only when the two societies are closer in political organization. All three issues – ethnic drowning in Tibet and Xingjiang, instability, terrorism, even drug trade across the western and southern borders from Xinjiang to Yunnan, and confrontation with Taiwan and embarrassments in Hong Kong – challenge China's role in the world today.

Tibet and Xinjiang A very important part of migration and cultural contact between China and beyond goes on across contiguous borders and with non-Han ethnic groups. These are 'ungrounded empires' of a different stripe – non-Han populations inside the PRC. The example that is of most concern to the PRC government is the connection of Xinjiang's Uighur population with the 'Stans,' or new states of Central Asia such as Kazakhstan and Kyrghyzstan, next door. Strong Turkic language identity and Islamic lifeways (including diet) define the Uighur population of this autonomous region, and increasing links with Kazakhs and others increase the identity of these communities – raising the real possibility that they will come to see themselves less as citizens of China as, potentially, of one of the neighboring states or as a state in and of themselves. Indeed, the same technologies of mass culture – cassettes of recorded music in the 1990s – have contributed to a resurgence of Uighur cultural identity in Xinjiang that has prompted reprisals by the Chinese state and continuing violence between Uighurs and Han authorities.[15] On the ground at China's border with, say, Burma or Kazakhstan, it is language, religion, and food which build everyday identity, and for minorities in those areas, that identity is not Chinese. It is for this reason that China has been so strict in maintaining sovereignty over Tibet – if it lets Tibet go independent, then why not Xinjiang, Inner Mongolia, the Korean counties of Manchuria, and the Thai areas of Yunnan? The PRC government is no more interested in real regional autonomy than European governments are interested in Basque, Catalan, or other nationality movements, or Canadian federal governments are in Quebec independence.

Tibet is probably not a viable modern nation-state, politically or economically. Tibet survived as a Central Asian kingdom during the period of European imperialism in the nineteenth century and came under the sway of Britain. Through the first half of the twentieth century it maintained autonomy, mostly because potential overlords, China or India, were weak and divided. The lamas ruled from Lhasa in an agriculturally based economy run by a theocratic state run on a shared Buddhist faith and culture. The coming of a renewed Chinese state in the early 1950s brought Chinese claims over Tibet – made by both the Qing Dynasty and the republic of Sun Yat-sen and Chiang Kai-shek – to Tibet's leaders. After a period of negotiations, the PRC asserted control by military invasion in 1959. The religious government fled to India and set up a government in exile in Daramsala. The Chinese government brought modern amenities, from increased electricity to public health improvements, but also brought Han chauvinism and intolerant secularism. What unity had existed in Tibet under the lamas dissolved as regional differences inside Tibet re-emerged and parts of Tibet were transferred to Sichuan and Qinghai provinces. Today, there is not a coherent Tibetan leadership. The exile leaders, and their children, are half-strangers to those who remained and endured Mao's campaigns and studied in Chinese schools. Yet Tibetan culture and identity endure and deserve autonomy and protection. But instant independence is unlikely to achieve this goal.

International declarations on Tibet distract world attention from the far more pressing danger of fighting in the Taiwan straits (as we shall see, below). More so, easy talk about getting China out of Tibet achieves little when it is limited to moral pronouncements that offer no workable solution. The PRC administration of Tibet is not good, not welcomed by Tibetans, and is a cause of justifiable international condemnation. Yet even the Dalai Lama is willing to accept autonomy within the PRC.[16] If we want to support a better life for Tibetans, it probably makes sense to follow the Dalai Lama's lead and promote compromise and negotiation. The PRC deserves embarrassment and international pressure for its neo-colonial attitudes, but it is well to remember that the PRC is doing what the US and European powers did not that long ago. It matters that we mention that when we criticize China; such humility defuses popular nationalist defensiveness and opens channels of productive consultations.

We should not forget the other examples of internal colonialism and Han-led ethnic drowning being carried out against Uighurs in Xinjiang and Mongols in Inner Mongolia. Ethnic drowning is the most controversial of Beijing's policies and has not received enough attention in the international press, though many commentators have noted it. For example, in Xinjiang, China's huge northwestern province, the Uighurs constituted over 80 percent of the population until the 1980s. Now they make up more like 40 percent of the population in their home areas. Massive in-migration of Han over the past twenty years threatens to drown not only Uighur culture in Xinjiang but Tibet, as well. The new Beijing–Lhasa express train line has just been completed in summer 2006. It will not only multiply the number of tourists at least tenfold but more importantly will also bring Han ethnic drowning to Tibet. Free Tibet may be a non-starter, as even the Dalai Lama acknowledges, but protecting autonomous Tibetan society within the PRC (and likewise for Uighur and other minority societies) is something worth fighting for. Here the experience of Canadian First Nations and Amerindians could serve as a fruitful starting point.

These are important problems, but not ones on which outsiders can be particularly effective.

Neighbors and strangers China's relations with its next-door neighbors are fragile, but recent efforts by the PRC state have achieved some results in building secure relations. Russia is China's most important next-door neighbor and former 'Elder Brother' and socialist bloc competitor. Two decades of dangerously strained relations came to an end in 1989, but were eclipsed by the events in Tiananmen. Today, relations with Russia are good. Putin and Hu Jintao, and their officials, meet regularly, particularly in the new Shanghai Cooperation Organization (SCO) that Russia and China lead to draw together the Central Asian states. The most recent meeting of the SCO in Shanghai in June 2006 underscored the increasing significance of this collaborative organization in trade and in diplomacy. A sure sign of the SCO's growing significance is the bitter complaints of US commentators that America has been left out. If Russia and China can continue to cooperate and to address the concerns of the smaller Central Asian states, then the SCO may well serve the trade and security roles that ASEAN or the Organization of American States have served.

Perched on the edge of China and Russia are Mongolia and North Korea. Each is fragile for different reasons. Mongolia has gone farthest in democratizing and is a darling of the American administration. It is also moderately stable and making headway economically. Mongolia plays a balancing role between Russia and China (which surround the country). China's biggest worries are getting rail line and gas pipeline right of ways negotiated through Mongolia. North Korea, on the other hand, is a major headache for China, but serves as a vivid reminder that a return to a Stalinist economy and polity is unthinkable. In fact, China has been responsible for moderating North Korean behavior in the Six Party Talks (including the USA and Russia, as well as neighbors) to defuse their nuclear program. The main threat to China from North Korea is, of course, that it may draw a major military confrontation with the USA to China's doorstep. Additionally, the breakdown of North Korea society has brought refugees and organized crime into China's northeastern provinces, where sizable Korean minority communities live.

In the southwest, on the Burmese border with Yunnan, the problem is not the militant separatists of Xinjiang or the geopolitical stress of North Korea but rather drugs and Aids. The military junta of Burma allows the famous Golden Triangle of opium production to carry on and black market groups inside China cheerfully participate. The border society is rife with prostitution and Aids transmission. These are problems the CCP is loath to talk about in public, and such official prudishness let Aids infection rates skyrocket before health activists and some local officials forced the Chinese government to acknowledge the problem and begin to address it. This border is an opportunity for Chinese cooperation with international NGOs and even with the United States – as all agree on the need to control the international drug trade and Aids.

Taiwan and Hong Kong The most dangerous policy of the PRC is that toward Taiwan. The topic is relatively well known (is Taiwan independent or not?) and gets formulaic news coverage that stresses the courage of democratic little Taiwan up against the giant communist China. There is, however, a very real danger of a shooting war over Taiwan, one that could drag both China and Asia into a terrible and needless conflagration. Hong Kong was supposed to serve as the trial run for a peaceful reunification but continued democratic agitation in the former British colony has not helped this cause.

Hong Kong returned to Chinese sovereignty in 1997. The port and city had been developed on the southeast China coast, at the mouth of the Pearl river just downstream from Guangzhou (Canton), in the 1840s by Britain. Britain had won 'the rock' of Hong Kong Island, and the tip of the Kowloon peninsula, as booty in the first Opium War in the Treaty of Nanjing in 1842. At the end of the century

Britain negotiated a hundred-year lease on the 'New Territories,' a much larger tract of land immediately to the north of Kowloon that made the colony viable in terms of water and food production. A century later the lease for the New Territories was up for renewal and the PRC wasn't interested. Margaret Thatcher negotiated the turnover of Hong Kong to PRC administration without much consultation with the residents of the colony – some 6 million Cantonese Chinese. Britain had run Hong Kong as a colony, but had run it pretty well. It was stable, prosperous, and emphatically under the rule of law. It was never a democracy under Britain until Britain had already signed it away to China. After the handover was negotiated in 1984 British authorities allowed limited democratization of the Hong Kong administration, to the fury of the Chinese government. Many people in Hong Kong took this preliminary democratization very seriously – they had been militating for it for years, anyway, but now they wanted a mechanism to enforce the guarantee in the handover agreement that Hong Kong's 'social system' would not be changed by the Beijing government for at least fifty years. The result has turned Hong Kong from a 'model' of reconciliation that would encourage Taiwan to 'come home' to a continuing embarrassment for the CCP. Hong Kong residents loudly and publicly supported the student demonstrators in Tiananmen in 1989 and have since then hit the streets to protest for implementation of the democratic legislative elections in Hong Kong provided for in the handover agreement. Hong Kong's chief executive is appointed by Beijing, not elected. Yet popular demonstrations drove the first chief executive, Tung Chee-hwa, from office. Donald Tsang, the current incumbent, is more moderate and careful to accommodate those demands. Leading Hong Kong politicians are not satisfied, however, and the embarrassments to Hu Jintao's administration continue. Most recently, Ms Anson Chan, the respected number two in Hong Kong before her retirement four years ago, has returned to the public arena to agitate for implementation of Hong Kong's promises of democratic legislative elections.[17] All this features in the international press and does nothing to encourage the Taiwanese to imperil their working electoral democracy by submitting to CCP rule.

Why is Taiwan so important to China's leaders? Why are they

willing to risk the stability so necessary for continued economic growth when they so clearly are willing to knuckle under to UN, WTO, and even US requirements on most other fronts? The story of Taiwan's history since the seventeenth century, when Han immigration began to dominate the aboriginal population of the island off the southeast coast of the China mainland, differs depending on whether you are in Beijing or Taipei. In China's version, Taiwan is just another part of China which for reasons of imperialist aggression has been temporarily cut off from home. First the Japanese 'won' the island in a war with China in 1895, and then the defeated nationalist government of Chiang Kai-shek fled to Taiwan and set up their government in exile when they were defeated by the CCP's armies in 1949. It is a point of pride to China's leaders to 'get Taiwan back' as the last momentous step back from a century of humiliation. As we have seen, nationalism is the main claim to legitimacy that the CCP government has in China today and Taiwan has become central to that claim. A Party leader can no more afford to be 'soft on Taiwan' than a US president can afford to be seen as 'soft on Cuba.'

The story on the other side of the Taiwan strait has the same facts but different conclusions. For most Taiwanese, Taiwan has clearly been a separate society for over a century. It has never been a part of the People's Republic of China. They feel about as Chinese as George Washington felt British – culturally yes, politically no. The problems go farther. When Chiang Kai-shek's nationalist government reoccupied Taiwan in 1945 after the defeat of the Japanese, the arrival of mainland troops was seen by many Taiwanese (even though they were Han with ancestors in Fujian province, across the straits) as an occupation by a foreign army. After all, those Taiwanese under the age of fifty had grown up in a colony of Japan, not China. Worse, the nationalist administration that came to Taiwan was not the best of Chiang Kai-shek's government. The best leaders and most disciplined troops were needed on the mainland to fight the civil war with the communists. From the start, Chinese rule of Taiwan was marked by maladministration, and in 1947 a massacre and political purge on a scale similar to that of Tiananmen in 1989. The 'February 28 Incident' of 1947 saw a savage repression of Taiwanese opposition by nationalist forces, who then forbade any further talk of the events. The entire nationalist government moved to Taiwan in 1949, making the island the Republic of China (in opposition to the mainland's People's Republic of China). For forty years 'Er-erba' (2-28) was a repressed secret in Taiwanese political life, and it was the belated admission and reversal of verdicts of Er-erba in the 1980s which contributed to the fall of the Nationalist Party (the KMT) and the rise of the Taiwanese Democratic Progressive Party which won the election in 2000 and rules Taiwan today under President Chen Sui-bian.

There is no easy reconciliation of these two histories. According to Guoguang Wu, the CCP needs the 'political capital' of diplomatic respect from Washington on the Taiwan question to buttress its domestic legitimacy inside China.[18] The wild card, however, has been the Chen Shui-bian administration in Taiwan. Chen's government continues to threaten to declare independence. This maddens the PRC authorities. It is a fatefully dangerous game. The most chilling comparative example of the power of shared ideology over rational-actor politics, of course, is the US war in Iraq. Even the US military didn't want to do it; ideology prevailed with tragedy for all concerned. It could happen to China and Taiwan. This is where the UN, well-meaning governments, the peace movement, and various friends of China and Taiwan need to concentrate their efforts – on the long, complex, frustrating, and ultimately profoundly important task of building peace across the Taiwan straits. According to most analysts, the solution lies in the illogical but humane policy of maintaining the status quo – wherein Taiwan's status as a polity is de jure left unsettled while de facto it carries on as an independent society and separate polity as it has for over a century.

China Rising: the international diplomacy of the PRC

In the context of the diverse social experience of globalization and the reality of popular nationalism as a major social response to the identity crisis of this 'globalization with Chinese characteristics,' the international diplomacy of the People's Republic of China appears just as frightening as the capitalist media's sensationalism, but for different reasons. Instead of a rehash of the nineteenth-century image of China as a sleeping dragon that will awaken to enslave us all to its opium-based despotism, China's threat to the world is that it might fail to address its roiling domestic challenges and thus implode, taking us with it into a maelstrom of out-of-control population growth, environmental destruction, and security nightmares. This negative scenario is not something the government of China is planning to bring about or even to threaten; it is their worst nightmare, as well as ours. China's leaders are no more saints than leaders in other countries, and they would prefer to stay in power and to enjoy the perquisites of their position, while at least some of them would hope, on balance, to do some good for China and the world.

The fact of China in the twenty-first century is this startling contradiction. China is arguably the greatest success story on the planet in the past thirty years. It is a stable, increasingly prosperous, and internationally responsible actor, the center of gravity for Asia and an anchor for stability and market prosperity. Yet China is also the ticking time bomb of unmanageable population, administrative corruption, environmental suicide, and thus of political and military instability when the stakes get too high or emotions get pushed to extremes.

From this perspective Western concerns about China Rising, China's blue-water navy, its claims to disputed territory in the South China Sea, etc., appear parochial indeed. These are the fears of old empires regretting the impending loss of their perquisites. The common facts are that China's government has 'played ball' with the West consistently since the 1980s on international issues – in the UN, with the WTO. Despite the fear-mongering in the commercial press and from our own politicians wishing to distract us from our domestic challenges, reform China has been a good neighbor internationally. Simple as that. Indeed, as we have seen, China has been too good a neighbor by refusing to protect its own citizens from the labor abuses of the neo-liberal globalized 'outsourcing' of sweatshop factories.

This is not the picture we get of China from the major Western media. Instead, we are told that China Rising is a threat to the US's military might, to Europe's economic balance, and to world energy resources. Headline after headline begins with suggestions that China's military expansion will lead to Chinese threats or actual attacks on the USA or other nations. China's multilateral relations since 1971, when the PRC took over the UN seat for China on the Security Council, do not, however, support such fear-mongering. It has been a responsible member of the UN, as well as an active participant in the full range of international institutions, treaties, and conventions.[19]

Relations with the USA have been bumpier, but since Nixon's rapprochement with Mao in 1972 the two nations have avoided a showdown.[20] The two biggest worries in recent years have been the 1999 bombing of the Chinese embassy in Belgrade by US planes and the April 2001 spy plane incident off the southeast coast of China. In both cases, despite hot rhetoric, the PRC avoided serious confrontation. In truth, both the US and Chinese administrations *in practice* reflect a commitment to continued even relations in order to reap the benefits of bilateral trade. The USA, however, remains China's single most important foreign partner – as much for America's huge market for Chinese manufactures as for the USA's formidable military establishment. The importance of the USA to China is shown by the PRC's tacit acceptance of American support for Taiwan – something the Chinese leadership bitterly resents, but knows cannot be helped at this time.

Second to its ties with the USA, China's relations with Japan and the EU are defined by similar economic interests and concerns, but with differing historical legacies. Europe is more or less off the hook for Britain's Opium War, replaced in the index of indignation by US insults and Japanese historical outrages. Still, on all these fronts the PRC's foreign policy of 'stability first' reigns supreme.[21] A particular success for PRC foreign policy has been relations with China's southern neighbors, the Association of Southeast Asian Nations (ASEAN). Careful efforts to calm concerns among Southeast Asian governments paid off in 2002 with an agreement establishing a China–ASEAN free trade area, and in October 2003 by China's accession to ASEAN's Treaty of Amity and Cooperation in Southeast Asia.[22]

In all, China Rising need not be a threat to world stability. The PRC government acts as a reasonable participant in the international order, but it is not the only Chinese actor, as we have seen. The forces and realities of the ungrounded empires of Overseas Chinese – who may or may not identify with the current government in Beijing – and of Cultural China also participate in defining China in the world and the world in China. Still, it is the PRC and the CCP leadership which has the 1.8-million-strong People's Liberation Army under its command. And Mao was not wrong in repeating the common saying of earlier years, 'Political power grows out of the barrel of a gun.' When it comes to the nation-state level of China's international relations, and particularly when it comes to the potential use of military force, only the Taiwan issue threatens to bring disaster in the form of military confrontation.

What will happen next?

While, of course, no one can predict the future because contingent acts – from 9/11 to tsunamis to election results – profoundly affect public life, the shape of economic and social life and the structures of political institutions both domestically and internationally strongly channel likely choices and actions. China is a capitalist one-party state with a dynamic economy and bleeding social sores of inequality and an environmental aneurism waiting to pop. It has a highly educated population that extends well beyond the nation-state borders and is connected by jet and Internet. It maintains a huge state and military apparatus to keep order. Its diverse population includes variant languages and cultures but is knit together by patriarchal family norms and a faith in a China Rising.

So the question is not 'what will happen next?' but 'what can you do?' Will we just watch a Leninist regime try to juggle the Three Chinas that Richard Madsen suggested – global economic leadership in its developed regions, social security and environmental clean-up in its rust-belt regions, and internal development aid to its Third World counties and regions? Chinese leaders and active citizens will have to undertake these tasks without the benefits of a liberal legal regime that protects individuals and civil society from state depredations and without the luxury of per capital levels of wealth enjoyed in more uniformly developed polities. Further, they will have to do these things in the face of unrestrained global capital interests, the power of multinational corporations, and a WTO regime that privileges rich, European, and North American-based companies and capitalist interests (private or state hardly matters) in Asia and China.

The surprise resource for people in China as they confront these problems and stark realities may well be the much-maligned Communist Party itself. Not because it is so wonderful, it is not; but because it is there, and at present there is no other practicable alternative nationwide, legal, moderately well-organized institution, aside from the military. Chinese leaders, since Mao, have chosen to keep the military under civilian control; they do so today, and are likely to continue this practice (exercised most recently by Hu Jintao through the administrative rotation of top generals to new subregions). What might this reformed CCP look like? That is truly beyond speculation, but if we imagine that this illiberal, formerly charismatic political organization is what people in China have to hand, then the state orientation of China's engaged intellectuals and the apparent passive acceptance of CCP dominance among China's entrepreneurial elite and middle classes are not signs of 'they're not getting it' (i.e. some inexplicable Chinese thick-headedness that makes them slow to pick up on the need for the rule of law and civil society), but are signs of the justly famous trait of practicality that observers of Chinese society have long noted.

One comparable case – useful for its differences as well as its similarities – is Mexico. In the 1980s Mexico's ruling party, the Institutional Revolutionary Party (PRI), also introduced sweeping neo-liberal economic reforms. In Mexico's case it was driven by the Latin American debt crisis, but the intention of the PRI paralleled the CCP's in many ways. Both were formerly charismatic one-party states suffering economic woes and political corruption. Both sought in neo-liberal economic reforms and engagement with world capital and trade to improve economic life and thereby secure their survival as one-party states. Thus, both Mexico and China sought market reform to avoid democracy, not to build it.[23] The differences between the two cases are important. Mexico is much smaller and utterly dependent on the USA. China can afford to negotiate more vigorously. Thus, Mexico sacrificed its sugar industry in order to get NAFTA through the US Congress (where Florida sugar interests threatened to bring down the vote).[24] China, on the other hand, has been able to negotiate significant protections for domestic growers in its accession to the WTO and it is clear, as McDonald's Corporation and others have learned, that when the social results of a contract cause Chinese leaders serious concern, they will not enforce the contract; China is a big enough economy and power that it can get concessions that Mexico cannot.

The Mexican comparison reminds us of the obvious: no foreign power can force the CCP to democratize, but the example of the PRI shows that neo-liberal reforms, while unable to deliver democracy and social justice, do set social forces in motion that can give the dispossessed a chance at getting some redress. We have seen the beginnings of these changes in reform China from labour demonstrations to public intellectuals to environmental semi-NGOs to local administrations in the richer areas. During my research trip in China during the spring and early summer of 2006 one thing struck me as I hacked through the polluted haze of Beijing – everyone was busy. For all the challenges that face people in China today, most of the people I met, from Beijing to Fujian, from university staff to cab drivers, from officials to dissidents, felt that they could work with what they have. Not that they are at all satisfied with the status quo (well, most of the officials seemed pretty comfortable), but they felt they had the tools to fight for change. As I have tried to outline in this book, I think they do, too.

Conclusion

The contemporary history of the present is dominated by two dates: 1989 and 11 September 2001. While 1989 is a very important year in the contemporary history of China, it is important not for the fall of communism – as it is in the broader world narrative of the collapse of the Soviet Union and its satellite states in eastern Europe – but for the survival of the Leninist regime in China. The popular protests and terrible military repression that are remembered as Tiananmen reflect the successful response of the CCP to a potent challenge, one that the CPSU and eastern European communist parties were unable to meet.

The military repression of students and workers around Tiananmen Square on 4 June 1989 and the campaign of arrests and prosecutions later in that year remain an unresolved issue in Chinese politics. Official China continues to claim this as a successful suppression of a 'counter-revolutionary rebellion' that has saved China from the dismal fate of Russia and the frightening wave of 'color revolutions' that have toppled authoritarian regimes across Eurasia in recent years. There is, however, a growing movement to reassess this official verdict. For some Chinese intellectuals (and even some officials), and certainly for most Western observers, Tiananmen stands as a symbol for *human rights abuses in China*. It stands for continuing repression of democratic party organizers, of citizen protest groups that get beyond the local level, and, most famously, the repression of the Falungong meditation group. As we have seen, Falungong was viewed by the CCP leadership more as an organizational threat than a religious or ideological concern. But Tiananmen and Falungong remain as reminders that while Chinese society has become less politically dominated since the current wave of reform and opening began in 1978, and more open to mobility of land, labor, and capital, it is not a polity characterized by the rule of law. The CCP runs a one-party state. And, while they wish to run it rationally and peaceably, they brook no competitors.

For many younger Chinese Tiananmen is a blank spot, not part of their experience and something they know 'we don't talk about.' This does not mean that Tiananmen is 'dead.' It is well to recall the example of the 'February 28 Incident' in Taiwan (see Chapter 6). It is a very comparable case of political repression, repressed political memory, and then the powerful political revival of that memory over a generation later. The same could happen with the memory of Tiananmen in China today, in five years, or ten or twenty. On 28 February 1947 KMT forces of the Chinese Nationalist government in Taiwan ruthlessly crushed a protest movement of dissatisfied Taiwanese seeking greater political rights. The repression was bloody and island-wide. Mention of it afterwards was forbidden and the ban was also ruthlessly enforced. When I first visited Taiwan in 1978 it was only whispered beyond my ears (and in Western history books not available in Taiwan). Nobody talked about it. Later, in the 1980s, public discussion grew. Then, unaccountably, some forty years after the event the outrages of 'Er-erba' (2-28) became a rallying cry of the opposition movement around the Democratic Progressive Party and indigenous Taiwanese politics. The revival of the memory of the 1947 repression and the failure of the KMT government to acknowledge and make reparations contributed to the political popularity of the Taiwanese Democratic Progressive Party, which won the presidency in 2000. [1] From South Africa to the Balkans to the Middle East, it is clear that some form of truth and reconciliation will come to pass; the choice for CCP leaders is only a matter of how and not whether Tiananmen will return to the center stage of Chinese political life. As long as Tiananmen remains a politically repressed memory it will serve as a metaphor to Chinese and to outsiders of the unmet promises of reform in China.

But to focus on Tiananmen and 1989 would be to distort life in China today. The student protestors and the man before the tank in 1989 are overshadowed in the lived experience of people in China today by the year 1992, the year the CCP irrevocably committed itself to 'socialism with Chinese characteristics' and 'market socialism.' Deng Xiaoping's Southern Tour in March 1992 set the authority of the last of the Long March veterans behind the market reforms under CCP authoritarian rule. This was then codified in the 14th Party Congress that October and the National People's Congress the following March. That reform program is the one that dominated Chinese life for the next decade, and it continues to operate in 2006.

September 11 2001 is not a critical date in the life of reform China, though as an active participant in the international regimes of collective security (as in the UN), economic cooperation (as in ASEAN and the WTO), and more generally in the globalized capitalist market (as in China's huge international trade and investment flows), China cannot avoid being affected by the fundamental changes in the world order under the War on Terror along with all other international actors. China has more leeway than many other states, however. Its size and economic clout, along with an intelligent and moderately coherent foreign policy establishment, allow the PRC to follow its own course in the age of American intervention. Thus, unlike Australia, which chooses to be America's deputy sheriff, or Canada, which endures marginalization for its unwillingness to take on that role, China can dip in and out of the Bush administration's 'coalition of the willing' without substantive penalty and turn the War on Terror to its own uses against minorities in western China. In trade relations, while the efforts of Chinese companies to buy American oil companies may be rebuffed, the USA has been unsuccessful in attempting to get the PRC to open the Chinese currency, the renminbi, to floating exchange rates. Meanwhile, Chinese banks finance a large and growing percentage of the US national debt. Again, 1992 is more important for putting China on its current path, and in the new century it is 2001, the year of China's entry into the WTO, which marks the next stage of that internationalizing journey.

Indeed, it is the specific gravity or sheer size of China, its economy, and its population which defines its role in the world. Given this political weight, the policy preferences of China's government and the cumulative effects of the life choices of farmers, workers, enterprises, and local governments matter hugely to the direction and health of the world. As we have seen, the PRC's foreign policy is essentially defensive. That does not mean it cannot or will not cause grave harm to regional security or to the operation of the world trade system. The case of Taiwan stands out: irrational feelings on both sides of the strait, shared by the leadership and significant portions of the populations in the mainland and on the island respectively, pose the greatest single likely cause of warfare in East Asia today. Beyond the Taiwan question, the PRC has a track record of pursuing its national interests by working through the international system, avoiding sharp conflict, and using negotiation. It also pursues them by seeking to catch up with the huge military arsenal of the USA. By 2010 China will have, by the estimate of most analysts, a credible blue-water navy. The intentions of China's current leadership are to use that navy to protect energy and trade lanes that China currently uses and to back up disputed claims for regional seabed areas in the East and South China seas. A conflagration over Taiwan would, however, quickly put that navy on a collision course with the United States forces in East Asia.

The potential for war is real. It would be a pointless disaster that any sane person would wish to avoid. Since such sanity, particularly among the US military and security establishment, did not stop America's tragic and counter-productive war in Iraq, one has to accept that the chances for war in the Taiwan strait are real and present. Peace between China and Taiwan has to be actively pursued with the energy that is currently lavished on the War on Terror. It is not simply a case of 'talking down' the irredentism of PRC ultra-nationalists, but also of counseling and rewarding pragmatic compromise among the political leaders of Taiwan. Since there is limited time and money for concerned individuals, state foreign affairs departments, and international organizations, we will have to prioritize. Between Free Tibet and peaceful Taiwan straits, the latter is the more urgent issue.

If Taiwan is the urgent problem (in the headlines), the social, economic, and environmental choices made by the diverse communities and myriad individuals in China constitute the most important arena (beyond the headlines) for the fate of the world. It is for this reason that I have focused on these aspects of China under reform. If not only the leadership but the various groups in China cannot address the needs of the swelling ranks of the dispossessed under reform, thereby failing to bring about a better level of social justice, if they cannot or will not improve the distribution of economic costs and benefits across social groups and so imperil China's ability to continue economic growth, or if they continue to ignore the environmental and energy disasters already apparent under current production practices, then real, long-term disaster awaits us all. For if China falls, Asia goes with it, and so in short order the economies, security, and environment of the Middle East, Africa, Europe and the Americas.

It has been the intention of this book to give the reader enough information about China to see where efforts may be most effective and where they may be of less use in addressing the compelling problems of the world as they affect China and as life in China affects those problems. The capitalist market is neither the primary cause of nor the final solution to abuses of people and places in China today. The Chinese Communist Party, likewise, is neither the primary cause of nor the ultimate solution for China's troubles. The most urgent challenge of China's diplomacy is less democratic dissidents or Tibet – which tend to make those of us in the West feel complacent and self-righteous – than the looming military disaster across the Taiwan straits, which should make us really worried, right now. The most important challenge to China's governance is sustainability, addressing the social justice claims of the losers of reform and addressing the unavoidable costs of averting China's slow-motion descent into environmental destruction.

Glorifying the market, demonizing Mao and the CCP, and privileging Free Tibet distract us from these fundamental problems of diplomacy and governance. Working for *fair trade* – rather than some unexamined 'free trade' – engaging in *real listening* to the interests of multiple Chinese communities, and working for *human security* for whole populations: these are worthwhile uses of our time in debate, in research, and in social and political action. The key to making these fine-sounding goals real is to put content behind 'fair,' 'real,' and 'human.' It is my hope that this book has provided something of that content – a beginning to an understanding of the issues of fairness, the reality of diverse voices, and the human role in the environment in the case of China.

Notes

Preface

1 An excellent account of the repression of Tiananmen is given in Timothy Brook, *Quelling the People: The Political Suppression of the Beijing Democracy Movement*, Stanford University Press, 1999. Brook estimates deaths in and around Tiananmen Square during the repression to be in the order of 300–500, but that deaths in Beijing surrounding the suppression were more likely 2,000–3,000.

2 For an account of contemporary Burma, see Christina Fink, *Living Silence: Burma under Military Rule*, London: Zed Books, 2001.

3 Harold Isaacs, *Scratches on Our Mind: American Views of China and India*, Armonk, NY: M. E. Sharpe, 1997 reprint.

4 Richard Madsen, 'China in the American Imagination,' *Dissent*, winter 1998, pp. 54–9, quote from p. 57.

5 Jeffrey Wasserstrom, 'Distortions in the China Debate,' *Dissent*, summer 1997, pp. 17–23, suggests the simple solution of *listening* to various Chinese voices more carefully.

6 This is the thesis of Elizabeth Perry's analysis in Jeffrey Wasserstrom and E. Perry (eds), *Popular Protest and Political Culture in China: Learning from 1989*, Boulder, CO: Westview Press, 1992, 2nd edn, 1994.

1 Making sense: what is 'China'?

1 Romila Thapar, *Early India: From the Origins to AD 1300*, Berkeley: University of California Press, 2004, and Sunil Khilnani, *The Idea of India*, New York: Farrar, Straus and Giroux, 1997.

2 China data come from <www.china.org.cn>, the government website. All three area estimates include large areas that are lightly inhabited – Greenland for Europe, Alaska for the USA, and the Qinghai-Tibet plateau for China.

3 Robert Benewick and Stephanie Donald, *The State of China Atlas*, Berkeley: University of California Press, 2005, p. 24. Data are for 2002.

4 John King Fairbank and Merle Goldman, *China: A New History*, Cambridge, MA: Harvard University Press, 1998, p. 10.

5 Ibid. A particularly enjoyable and reliable general history is provided by Patricia Ebrey, *The Cambridge Illustrated History of China*, Cambridge University Press, 1999.

6 Jonathan Spence, *The Chan's Great Continent: China in Western*

Minds, New York: W. W. Norton, 1999, and Andre Gunder Franke, *Reorient: Global Economy in the Asian Age*, Berkeley: University of California Press, 1998.

7 Another mission in 1816 under Lord Amherst met a similar fate. See Fairbank and Goldman, *China: A New History*, pp. 196ff.

8 Details can be found in Susan Blum, 'China's many faces, ethnic, cultural, and religious pluralism,' in Timothy B. Weston and Lionel M. Jensen (eds), *China Beyond the Headlines*, Lanham, MD: Rowman & Littlefield, 2000, and Blum, *Portraits of 'Primitives': Human Kinds in the Chinese Nation*, Lanham, MD: Rowman & Littlefield, 2000.

9 Blum, 'China's many faces', pp. 69–95.

10 The Chinese word for ethnicity is *minzu*. It is the criterion for both legal and popular understandings of identity and difference among culture groups. The criteria, borrowed from the Soviet Union, for an ethnic group are: common territory, common language, common economic life, common psychological (cultural) life. In contrast to European practice, ethnicity is not assumed to be biological or racial. Shared history and current practice define the community and the individual identity as a member within it. See Fei Hsiao-tung, 'Ethnic identification in China,' trans. Wang Huimin and Wu Zenfang, *Social Sciences in China*, 1, March 1980, pp. 94–107.

11 Xiaolin Guo, 'Land expropriations and rural conflicts in China,' *China Quarterly*, 166, 2001, pp. 422–39.

12 June Teufel Dreyer, *China's Forty Millions: Minority Nationalities and National Integration in the People's Republic of China*, Cambridge, MA: Harvard University Press, 1976.

13 Jay Dautcher, 'Reading out-of-print: popular culture and protest on China's western frontier,' in Weston and Jensen, *China's Transformations*, pp. 273–94.

14 Jack Hayes, '*Jig rTen* – a shift in worlds: the state, society and environment in northern Sichuan wildlands, 1880–2000,' PhD dissertation, University of British Columbia, November 2006.

15 Tony Saich, *Governance and Politics of China*, London: Palgrave, 2001, pp. 5–6.

16 On Buddhist and Daoist estimates, see Blum, 'China's many faces,' p. 88; for other religions, see the excellent collection of essays in the special issue of the *China Quarterly* (174, June 2003) on 'Religion in China today,' edited by Daniel Overmyer; data from pp. 453, 468, 491.

17 Jason Kindopp and Carol Lee Hamrin (eds), *God and Caesar in China: Policy Implications of Church–State Tensions*, Washington, DC: Brookings Institution, 2004.

18 Arthur Wolf (ed.), *Religion and Ritual in Chinese Society*, Stanford, CA: Stanford University Press, 1999.

19 David Ownby, *Falungong and China's Future*, Boulder, CO: Rowman and Littlefield, forthcoming.

20 Patricia M. Thornton, 'The new cybersects,' in Elizabeth J. Perry and Mark Selden (eds), *Chinese Society: Change, Conflict and Resistance*, 2nd edn, London: Routledge, 2003, pp. 247–70.

21 Saich, *Governance*, p. 10.

22 Ching Kwan Lee, *Gender and the South China Miracle: Two Worlds of Factory Women*, Berkeley: University of California Press, 1998; Tamara Jacka, *Rural Women in Urban China: Gender, Migration and Social Change*, Armonk, NY: M. E. Sharpe, 2005.

23 For short and evocative portrayals of these issues, see Harriet Evans, 'Marketing femininity: images of the modern Chinese woman,' in Weston and Jensen, *China Beyond the Headlines*, 2000, pp. 217–44, and essays by Wang Zheng, 'Gender, employment and women's resistance,' and Tyrene White, 'Domination, resistance and accommodation in China's one-child campaign,' in Perry and Selden, *Chinese Society*, pp. 158–203.

24 Tiejun Cheng and Mark Selden, 'City, countryside and the dialectics of control. The origins of China's hukou system, 1949–1960,' *China Quarterly*, 139, Fall 1994.

25 Xiaobo Lü and Elizabeth Perry (eds), *Danwei: The Changing Chinese Workplace in Historical and Comparative Perspective*, Armonk, NY: M. E. Sharpe, 1997.

26 Hein Mallee, 'Migration, *hukou* and resistance in reform China,' in Perry and Selden, *Chinese Society*, pp. 136–57.

27 Ching Cheong and Ching Hung Yee, *Handbook and China's WTO Accession and Its Impacts*, Singapore: World Scientific Publishing Company, 2003.

28 This count goes by *administrative level*, so cities at the county level count with counties, and autonomous regions at the provincial level count with provinces.

29 Much of this information for 2004 can be found in the CCP and PRC constitutions: <www.china.org.cn/english/features/49109.htm> and <www.china.org.cn/english/Political/25060.htm>, accessed 10 March 2006. The root webpage, <www.china.org.cn> is a good source of English-language information and statistics from the PRC government. A good introduction is given by Saich, *Governance*.

30 This example of 'two states' comes from Guo Xiaolin.

2 Living history: what was Maoism?

1 I have coined 'actually existing Maoism,' to borrow from Vaclav Havel's depiction in the 1980s of 'actually existing socialism' in eastern Europe, to suggest the parallel experience of dissonance for a generation raised on the ideals of socialism but subjected to the terrors of Stalinist state socialism.

2 See Stephen Lovell, *Destination in Doubt: Russia since 1989*, London: Zed Books, 2006.

3 Mao studies are a thriving cottage industry in academia. Stuart Schram remains the doyen of serious Mao students; see his *The Thought of Mao Zedong*, Cambridge: Cambridge University Press, 1989. A number of good biographies echo Schram's balanced assessment of Mao's strengths and weakness, such as Jonathan Spence, *Mao*, Penguin, 1999. A documentary history that seeks to make a critical assessment of Mao's contributions and some of the scholarly literature is Timothy Cheek, *Mao Zedong and China's Revolutions*, Boston, MA: Bedford Books, 2002.

4 Jonathan Spence, *God's Chinese Son: The Taiping Heavenly Kingdom of Hong Xiuquan*, NY: W. W. Norton, 1996.

5 Mao Zedong, 'On New Democracy,' can be found in his standard *Selected Works of Mao Tse-tung* published in Beijing and available on-line at: <www.marxists.org/reference/archive/mao/>; also Cheek, *Mao Zedong*, p. 80.

6 Roderick MacFarquhar, *Origins of the Cultural Revolution*, vol. I, NY: Columbia University Press, 1974.

7 Frederick Teiwes with Warren Sun, *China's Road to Disaster*, Armonk, NY: M. E. Sharpe, 1998; MacFarquhar, *Origins*, vol. II, NY: Columbia University Press, 1986.

8 Estimates of deaths stemming from the Great Leap range from 20 to 30 million. Deng Xiaoping admitted to tens of millions of needless deaths from the 1959–61 post-Leap famine. See details in MacFarquhar and Teiwes and Sun, note 7 above, and Jasper Becker, *Hungry Ghosts: Mao's Secret Famine*, NY: Free Press, 1996.

9 Dali L. Yang, *Calamity and Reform in China: State, Rural Society and Institutional Change Since the Great Leap Famine*, Stanford, CA: Stanford University Press, 1996.

10 Zhou Enlai promoted the focus on 'modern agriculture, industry, national defense, and science and technology' in his work report to the 3rd National People's Congress in December 1964. Frederick Teiwes convincingly argues that it was Mao Zedong himself who put the slogan of 'Four Modernizations' forward at the time and that Zhou was simply promoting the Chairman's policy. Mao had mixed feelings, however, and abandoned the modernization program in favor of class struggle, while Zhou and the Party bureaucracy returned to the modernization program again in the 1975 NPC session, when Deng Xiaoping was first returned to leadership, and again in the post-Mao period. See Frederick C. Teiwes, *Politics and Purges in China*, Armonk, NY: M. E. Sharpe, 2nd edn, 1993, pp. 438, 485.

11 There is a huge literature on the Cultural Revolution, both academic and personal. The works of MacFarquhar and Teiwes, cited above, give the high politics. Roderick MacFarquhar and Michael Schoenhals provide a fresh history, including more of the 'life on the ground,' in *Mao's Last Revution*, Cambridge, MA: Harvard University Press, 2006. Schoenhals also provides an excellent set of documents, *China's Cultural Revolution, 1966–1969: Not a Dinner Party*, Armonk, NY: M. E. Sharpe, 1996. Of the

dozens of memoirs of former Red Guards, I find to be particularly insight-ful Rae Yang, *Spider Eaters: A Memoir* (Berkeley: University of California Press, 1997).

12 Wang Yi, under the pen-name Xin Yuan, 'A place in the pantheon: Mao and folk religion,' published in Chinese in Hong Kong in 1992 and translated by Geremie Barmé in *Shades of Mao: The Posthumous Cult of the Great Leader*, Armonk, NY: M. E. Sharpe, 1996, pp. 197–8.

13 Original Party texts are translated and carefully analysed by Gang Lin, 'Ideology and political institutions for a new era,' in Gang Lin and Xiaobo Hu (eds), *China after Jiang*, Stanford, CA: Stanford University Press, 2003, pp. 39–68, quote from p. 39.

14 Ibid., p. 44.

15 Lin Yunshan, 'Strengthening, expanding, and innovating in propaganda and ideological work in accordance with the requirements of constructing a harmonious socialist society,' *Qiushi*, 19, 2005, translated in FBIS-CHI (Foreign Broadcast Information Service, US Government), 1 October 2005.

16 Joseph Kahn, 'Sharp debate erupts in China over socialism and capitalism,' *New York Times*, 12 March 2006, p. 1.

17 Suisheng Zhao, *A Nation-State by Construction: Dynamics of Modern Chinese Nationalism*, Stanford, CA: Stanford University Press, 2004; Peter Hays Gries, *China's New Nationalism: Pride, Politics, and Diplomacy*, Berkeley: University of California Press, 2004.

18 Merle Goldman has chronicled this history in her books since 1967. Her views are summarized nicely in the chapters on ideology and intellectuals for the *Cambridge History of China* that are reproduced in Merle Goldman and Leo Ou-Fan Lee (eds), *An Intellectual History of Modern China*, Cambridge: Cambridge University Press, 2002.

19 Wenfang Tang, *Public Opinion and Political Change in China*, Stanford, CA: Stanford University Press, 2005, p. 187.

20 Elizabeth Perry, 'Introduction: The changing Chinese workplace in historical and comparative perspective,' in Xiaobo Lü and Elizabeth Perry (eds), *Danwei: The Changing Chinese Workplace in Historical and Compara-tive Perspective*, Armonk, NY: M. E. Sharpe, 1997, pp. 5–6.

21 Suisheng Zhao, *A Nation-State by Construction*.

22 Geremie Barmé, *In the Red: Contemporary Chinese Culture*, New York: Columbia University Press, 1999, p. 334.

23 Jung Chang and Jon Halliday, *Mao: The Unknown Story*, London: Jonathan Cape, 2005. This biography has been warmly embraced by journalists and roundly criticized by scholars. A useful array of special-ist criticism appears in *The China Journal*, Canberra, 55, January 2006, pp. 95–139, as well as in Jonathan Spence's rueful review in the *New York Review of Books*, 4 November 2005.

24 Xu Jilin, 'The fate of an enlightenment: twenty years in the Chinese

intellectual sphere (1978–1998),' pp. 183–203, and Geremie R. Barmé and Gloria Davies, 'Have we been noticed yet? Intellectual contestation and the Chinese web,' pp. 75–108, both in Edward Gu and Merle Goldman (eds), *Chinese Intellectuals between State and Market*, London: Routledge, 2004.

3 Reform: Mao is dead, long live Mao!

1 The official English-language version appears in *Beijing Review*, 6 July 1981, pp. 10–39. For a fascinating example of the continued balancing act the CCP plays in refuting the Cultural Revolution while trying to maintain Mao as the source of Party legitimacy, see the selections of the 1981 Historical Resolution as they are presented on the webpage of the International Department of the Party: <www.idcpc.org.cn/english/maozedong/comments.htm>.

2 See Michael Schoenhals, 'Is the "Cultural Revolution" Really Necessary?,' in Werner Draguhn and David S. G. Goodman (eds), *China's Communist Revolutions: Fifty Years of the People's Republic of China*, London: RoutledgeCurzon, 2002, pp. 159–76. Schoenhals' title is corrected based on personal correspondence; the printed version erroneously gives the title as 'Was the Cultural Revolution … '; see p. 176 for the author's main point, which is that the use of the term 'Cultural Revolution' obscures the roots of reform more than it illuminates them. See also Marie-Claire Bergere's chapter, 'China in the wake of the communist revolution: social transformations, 1949–1966,' pp. 98–123 in the same volume.

3 Maurice Meisner gives a thoughtful assessment of these developments from a Marxist perspective in *The Deng Xiaoping Era: An Inquiry into the Fate of Chinese Socialism, 1978–1994*, NY: Hill & Wang, 1996.

4 An excellent and detailed survey of these reforms is given in Tony Saich, *Governance and Politics of China*, London: Palgrave, 2001, ch. 3.

5 For an account of Wei Jingsheng's efforts which places him in a narrative that emphasizes dissidents and democrats in China, see John Gittings, *The Changing Face of China: From Mao to Market*, NY: Oxford University Press, 2005, pp. 140–63.

6 Merle Goldman, Timothy Cheek, and Carol Hamrin (eds), *China's Intellectuals and the State: The Search for a New Relationship*, Cambridge, MA: Harvard Contemporary China Series 1989, and B. Brugger and D. Kelly, *Chinese Marxism in the Post-Mao Era*, Stanford, CA: Stanford University Press, 1991.

7 Barry Naughton, *Growing Out of the Plan: Chinese Economic Reform, 1978–1993*, NY: Cambridge University Press, 1995, pp. 175–6.

8 Pitman Potter, *From Leninist Discipline to Socialist Legalism: Peng Zhen on Law and Political Authority in the PRC*, Stanford, CA: Stanford University Press, 20003.

9 David Shambaugh, *Modernizing China's Military: Progress, Problems, and Prospects*, Berkeley: University of California Press, 2004.

10 James H. Williams, 'Fang Lizhi's expanding universe,' *China*

Quarterly, 123, 1990, pp. 458–83; Fang Lizhi, *Bringing Down the Great Wall: Writings on Science, Culture and Democracy in China*, trans. James H. Williams, NY: W. W. Norton, 1992.

11 In fact, the Party's fears were overblown: the students did not want the workers to participate in their elite protest. See Elizabeth J. Perry, 'Casting a Chinese "democracy" movement: the roles of students, workers, and entrepreneurs,' in Jeffrey N. Wasserstrom and Elizabeth J. Perry (eds), *Popular Protest and Political Culture in Modern China: Learning from Tiananmen*, Boulder, CO: Westview Press, 1992, pp. 146–64.

4 Brave new world: reform and openness

1 Timothy Brook and Rene Wagner, 'The teaching of history to foreign students at Peking University,' *China Quarterly*, 71, September 1977, pp. 598–607.

2 Geremie Barmé, 'To screw foreigners is patriotic,' in Barmé, *In the Red: On Contemporary Chinese Culture*, NY: Columbia University Press, 1999, p. 255. Barmé is taking the racialized sexual patriotism of his title from the comments of a Chinese prostitute reported in Sang Ye, *The Year the Dragon Came*, Brisbane: Queensland University Press, 1996, p. 14.

3 Yuezhi Zhao, *Media, Market, and Democracy in China: Between the Party Line and the Bottom Line*, Champaign: University of Illinois Press, 1998; Stephanie H. Donald, Michael Keane and Yin Hong (eds), *Media in China: Consumption, Content, and Crisis*, London: RoutledgeCurzon, 2002.

4 John Friedmann, *China's Urban Transition*, Minneapolis: University of Minnesota Press, 2005, esp. ch. 1; Jacob Eyferth (ed.), *How China Works: Perspectives on the Twentieth-century Workplace*, London: Routledge, 2006.

5 See ch. 1, above.

6 'Mixed Memories of "Zhiqing,"' *China Daily*, 15 June 2004, accessed at <www.chinadaily.com.cn/english>, 14 March 2006; Maurice Meisner, *Mao's China and After*, 3rd edn, NY: Free Press, 1999; B. Michael Frolic, *Mao's People: Sixteen Portraits of Life in Revolutionary China*, Cambridge, MA: Harvard University Press, 2005.

7 *China Statistical Yearbook*, 1999, cited in Tony Saich, *Governance and Politics of China*, London: Palgrave, 2001, p. 150.

8 David Zweig, *Freeing China's Farmers: Rural Restructuring in the Reform Era*, Armonk, NY: M. E. Sharpe, 1997.

9 Susan Blum, 'Rural China and the WTO,' *Journal of Contemporary China*, 11(32), 2002, p. 472.

10 Peter Ho, 'Contesting rural spaces: land disputes, customary tenure and the state,' and David Zweig, 'To the courts or to the barricades: can new political institutions manage rural conflict?,' in Elizabeth J. Perry and Mark Selden (eds), *Chinese Society: Change, Conflict and Resistance*, 2nd edn, London: Routledge, 2003, pp. 93–135.

11 Saich, *Governance*, p. 75.

12 'Chairman Mao's ark: one of the floating population,' in Sang Ye, *China Candid: The People on the People's Republic*, Berkeley: University of California Press, 2006, p. 28.

13 Robert Benewick and Stephanie Donald, *The State of China Atlas*, Berkeley: University of California Press, 2005, p. 17.

14 Timothy B. Weston, 'China's labor woes: will the workers crash the party?,' in Timothy B. Weston and Lionel M. Jensen, *China Beyond the Headlines*, Lanham, MD: Rowman & Littlefield, 2000, pp. 254–74.

15 Antia Chan and Hongze Wang, 'The impact of the state on workers' conditions comparing Taiwanese factories in China and Vietnam,' *Pacific Affairs*, 77(4), Winter 2004/05, pp. 629–46.

16 Sing Lee and Arthur Kleinman, 'Suicide as resistance in Chinese society,' in Perry and Selden, *Chinese Society*, pp. 289–311.

17 Benewick and Donald, *The State of China Atlas*, p. 29.

18 Jack Patrick Hayes, '*Jig rTen* – a shift in worlds: the state, society and environment in northern Sichuan wildlands, 1880–2000,' PhD dissertation, University of British Columbia, 2006; Xiaolin Guo, 'Land expropriation and rural conflict in China,' *China Quarterly*, 166, 2001, pp. 422–39.

19 Dorothy Solinger, 'Why we cannot count the "unemployed,"' *China Quarterly*, 167, September 2001, pp. 671–88.

20 Reported in the Hong Kong journal *Zhengming*, in April 1993, this case is analyzed in Ching Kwan Lee, 'Pathways of labor insurgency,' in Perry and Selden, *Chinese Society*, p. 80.

21 *China Daily*, 29 April 2002. Counting these largely unregistered migrant laborers has to be a matter of estimation, but most scholars accept the 130–160 million range for 2005.

22 Rachel Murphy, *How Migrant Labor is Changing Rural China*, NY: Cambridge University Press, 2002.

23 For studies of dissidents, as well as those who work with the system, see Merle Goldman, *From Comrade to Citizen: The Struggle for Political Rights in China*, Cambridge, MA: Harvard University Press, 2005.

24 Wenfang Tang, *Public Opinion and Political Change in China*, Stanford, CA: Stanford University Press, 2005, p. 162.

25 Zhu Yong (ed.), *Zhishifenzi yinggai ganshenma?* [What should intellectuals do?], Beijing: Shishi chubanshe,1999, p. 1. Zhu Yong is a noted younger (born 1968) essay writer and editor in Beijing who reflects on intellectual issues and changes. See also his collection *Liushiniandai jiyi* [Recollections of the sixties], Beijing: Zhongguo wenlian chubanshe, 2002.

26 This section draws from Timothy Cheek, 'The new Chinese intellectual: Globalised, disoriented, reoriented,' in Timothy B. Weston and Lionel M. Jensen (eds), *China's Tranformations: The Stories Beyond the Headlines*, Lanham, MD: Rowman & Littlefield, 2006, rev. edn.

27 See, for example, his collection of essays, *Lilun yu xinzhi* [Knowledge and wisdom], Nanjing: Jiangsu renmin chubanshe, 2001.

28 See Liu Dong, 'Revisiting the perils of "designer pidgin scholarship"', in Gloria Davies, *Voicing Concerns: Contemporary Chinese Critical Enquiry*, Boulder, CO: Rowman & Littlefield, 2001, pp. 87–108, and interview with author, Vancouver, October 2003.

29 Century China can be accessed on the Web at: <www.cc.org.cn>.

30 See, for example, Xu Jilin, 'The fate of an enlightenment: twenty years in the Chinese intellectual sphere (1978–98),' in Edward Gu and Merle Goldman, *China's Intellectuals between State and Market*, London: Routledge, 2004, pp. 183–203.

31 Professor Xu and I co-organized one of those conferences, in December 2002, on 'Public intellectuals in China.'

32 There have been notable Chinese scholars studying and working in Western societies since at least the 1910s. Such scholars were, however, few in number. The 1980s brought not tens but tens of thousands of Chinese scholars to study and work in the West, and it is this *quantity* of Chinese scholars now in Western societies which has contributed to the changed *quality* of 'Western' scholarship today.

33 Yanqi Tong, *Transitions from State Socialism: Economic and Political Change in Hungary and China*, Lanham, MD: Rowman & Littlefield, 1997; Yuezhi Zhao, *Media, Market, and Democracy in China: Between the Party Line and the Bottom Line*, Urbana: University of Illinois Press, 1998; Suisheng Zhao (ed.), *China and Democracy*, London: Routledge, 2000.

34 This interview with the NPC delegate appears as 'The people's deputy: a congresswoman,' in Sang Ye, *China Candid: The People on the People's Republic*, Berkeley: University of California Press, 2006, pp. 73–84, quotes from p. 79.

35 Wenfang Tang, *Public Opinion and Political Change in China*, Stanford, CA: Stanford University Press, 2005, p. 187.

36 Richard Madsen, 'One country, three systems: state–society relations in post-Jiang China,' in Gang Lin and Xiaobo Hu (eds), *China after Jiang*, Stanford, CA: Stanford University Press, 2003, pp. 91–114, this quote from p. 92.

37 Ibid., p. 94.

38 Ibid., p. 100.

39 Ibid., p. 102.

40 Ibid., p. 109.

41 A good collection of his articles on China's environment from over the years is given in Vaclav Smil, *China's Past, China's Future*, in the Critical Asian Studies Series, London: Routledge, 2003. Smil's famous books include *The Bad Earth* (1984) and *China's Environmental Crisis* (1993).

42 Elizabeth C. Economy, *The River Runs Black: The Environmental Challenge to China's Future*, Ithaca, NY: Cornell University Press, 2004, p. 25. The list of environmental troubles draws from Economy's summary, pp. 9–10, and recaps data presented in Vaclav Smil's books.

5 Winners and losers: reactions to reform

1 Richard McGregor, 'New breed of fixers in Chinese struggle for rights,' *Financial Times*, 15 February 2006.

2 See Hu Jintao's speech to the Fortune 500 Global Forum in Beijing, *China Daily*, 17 May 2005, accessed at <www.chinadaily.com.cn/english/doc/2006-01/27/content_516221.htm>.

3 Yuezhi Zhao, 'Underdogs, lapdogs and watchdogs: journalists and the public sphere problematic in China,' in Edward Gu and Merle Goldman, *Chinese Intellectuals between State and Market*, London: Routledge, 2004, pp. 43–74.

4 Described in Elizabeth C. Economy, *The River Runs Black: The Environmental Challenge to China's Future*, Ithaca, NY: Cornell University Press, 2004, pp. 146–9.

5 Reported in *Far Eastern Economic Review*, 26 June 1997, p. 15, as presented in Lee, 'Pathways of labour insurgency,' in Elizabeth J. Perry and Mark Selden (eds), *Chinese Society: Change, Conflict and Resistance*, 2nd edn, London: Routledge, 2003, p. 81.

6 Kevin J. O'Brien and Li Lianjiang, *Rightful Resistance in Rural China*, NY: Cambridge University Press, 2006.

7 Susan Brownell and Jeffrey N. Wasserstrom (eds), *Chinese Feminities/Chinese Masculinities: A Reader*, Berkeley: University of California Press, 2002.

8 As has been cogently argued by Bruce Dickson in 'Populist authoritarianism: the future of the Chinese Communist Party,' at the conference 'Behind the Bamboo Curtain: Chinese leadership, politics and policy,' 2 November 2005, from the China Vitae website, <www.chinavitae.com/index.php>.

9 Cheng Li, 'One party, two factions: Chinese bipartisanship in the making?,' 2 November 2005, at the conference, 'Behind the Bamboo Curtain: Chinese Leadership, Politics and Policy,' from the China Vitae website, <www.chinavitae.com/index.php>; Cheng Li, *China's Leaders: The New Generation*, Lanham, MD: Rowman & Littlefield, 2001.

10 Kenneth W. Foster, 'Improving municipal governance in China: Yantai's pathbreaking experiment in administrative reform,' *Modern China*, 32(2), April 2006, pp. 1–30.

11 Dali L. Yang, *Remaking the Chinese Leviathan: Market Transition and the Politics of Governance in China*, Stanford, CA: Stanford University Press, 2004, quote from p. 18.

12 Bruce Dickson, *Red Capitalists in China: The Party, Private Entrepreneurs, and Prospects for Political Change*, NY: Cambridge University Press, 2003.

13 Joseph Fewsmith, 'Where do correct ideas come from? – the party school, key think tanks, and the intellectuals,' in David M. Finkelstein and Maryanne Kivlehan (eds), *China's Leadership in the 21st Century: The Rise*

of the Fourth Generation, Armonk, NY: M. E. Sharpe, 2003; Yuezhi Zhao, 'Underdogs.'

14 'Yingxiang Zhongguo gonggong zhishifenzi 50 ren,' *Nanfang renwu zhoukan* [Southern People Weekly], September 2004, <http://business. sohu.com/s2004/zhishifenzi50.shtml> (accessed 15 March 2006). David Kelly gives a good assessment of this list and the political fallout it generated in autumn 2004 in 'The importance of being public,' *China Review*, 31, 2004/05, pp. 28–37.

15 Falungong (which also calls itself 'Falun dafa') is covered in nearly every book on contemporary China and it maintains its own propaganda network; see <www.faluninfo.net/>. For a serious analysis of Falungong from the perspective of China's social history, see David Ownby, *Falungong and China's Future* (forthcoming).

16 Steven Levitsky, *Transforming Labor-based Parties in Latin America: Argentine Peronism in Comparative Perspective*, NY: Cambridge University Press, 2003.

17 Robert Benewick and Stephanie Donald, *The State of China Atlas*, Berkeley: University of California Press, 2005, pp. 88–91.

18 For a description of SEPA duties, see 'Website of Chinese State Environmental Protection Administration' at <http://www.sepa.gov.cn/english/>.

19 Jonathan Schwartz, 'Environmental NGOs in China: roles and limits,' *Pacific Affairs*, 77(1), 2004, pp. 28–49.

20 Tim Oakes, *Tourism and Modernity in China*, London: Routledge, 1998.

21 See Hu Jintao's speech to the Fortune 500 Global Forum in Beijing, *China Daily*, 17 May 2005, accessed at <www.chinadaily.com.cn/english/doc/2006-01/27/content_516221.htm>.

22 Anders Stephanson, *Manifest Destiny: American Expansion and the Empire of Right*, NY: Hill & Wang, 1995; Seymour Martin Lipset, *American Exceptionalism: A Double-edged Sword*, NY: W. W. Norton, 1997. The complex role of 'the missionary dimension of American foreign policy' and state interests, of course, continues under the Bush administration and the War on Terror; see Nicholas Guyatt, *Another American Century? The United States and the World since 9/11*, London: Zed Books, 2003, esp. pp. 254ff.

23 Suisheng Zhao, 'Chinese intellectuals' quest for national greatness and nationalistic writings in the 1990s,' *China Quarterly*, 152, 1997, pp. 725–45. See also Zhao's longer study, *A Nation-State by Construction: Dynamics of Modern Chinese Nationalism*, Stanford, CA: Stanford University Press.

24 Reinhart Koselleck explores the role of such enduring concepts in *Futures Past: On the Semantics of Historical Time*, Cambridge, MA: MIT Press, 1985.

25 The best review for my money is Suisheng Zhao, *A Nation-State by*

Construction: Dynamics of Modern Chinese Nationalism, Stanford, CA: Stanford University Press, 2004.

26 This well-known website's Chinese address is: <http://zh.wikipedia. org/wiki/首页>, accessed 19 March 2006.

27 Philip P. Pan, 'Reference tool on Web finds fans, censors,' *Washington Post Foreign Service*, 20 February 2006, p. A01.

28 Liu Xiaobo, 'Wo yu hulianwang,' Beijing, 14 February 2006, translated by David Cowhig from the ESWN blogger, Roland Song, <www. zonaeuropa.com/20060224_2.htm> (accessed 19 March 2006).

29 My own observation of a bumper sticker in Hayes, KS; Richard Madsen, 'China in the American imagination,' *Dissent*, Winter 1998, p. 55.

6 China in the world today

1 James L. Watson, 'China's Big Mac attack,' *Foreign Affairs*, May/June 2000, p. 120.

2 Gungwu Wang (ed.), *Community and Nation: China, Southeast Asia, and Australia*, St Leonards, Australia: Allen & Unwin, 1992, p. 3. More generally, Lynn Pan (ed.), *The Encyclopedia of the Overseas Chinese*, Singapore: Archipelago Press, 1998.

3 Aihwa Ong and Donald Nonini (eds), *Ungrounded Empires: The Cultural Politics of Modern Chinese Transnationalism*, London: Routledge, 1996.

4 Gaungwu Wang, *Community and Nation*, pp. 6–7.

5 Aihwa Ong, *Flexible Citizenship: The Cultural Logics of Transnationality*, Durham, NC: Duke University Press, 1999. By definition a Canadian or Jamaican citizen cannot be Chinese; it is still the case that a PRC-born Chinese citizen must relinquish their passport and citizenship when taking on a new citizenship.

6 The role of the sweet potato and maize, as well as other factors such as the peace enforced by the Qing and the control of smallpox, are discussed in John King Fairbank and Merle Goldman, *China: A New History*, Cambridge, MA: Cambridge University Press, 1999, pp. 168–9.

7 Iris Chang, *Thread of the Silkworm*, NY: Basic Books, 1996. Qian's name is given in the old Romanization in this book as Tsien Hsue-shen.

8 Timothy Cheek, 'Xu Jilin and the thought work of China's public intellectuals,' *China Quarterly*, 186, June 2006, pp. 401–20.

9 Tu Wei-ming, 'Cultural China: the periphery as the center,' *Daedalus*, Spring 1991, pp. 1–32.

10 Henry Rosemont, Jr, *A Chinese Mirror*, La Salle, IL: Open Court, 1991. Rosemont also produced with Roger T. Ames *The Analects of Confucius: A Philosophical Translation*, NY: Ballantine Books, 1998.

11 Unsurprisingly, this youth-oriented genre is well represented on the Web. For an introduction (in English) to the world of Cantopop, try: <www. answers.com/topic/cantopop>.

12 Andrew F. Jones, *Like a Knife: Ideology and Genre in Contemporary Chinese Popular Music*, Ithaca, NY: Cornell University Press, 1992.

13 Special issue of *China Information* (Leiden), 2002; Christopher R. Hughes and Gundrun Wacker (eds), *China and the Internet: Politics of the Digital Leap Forward*, London: RoutledgeCurzon, 2003.

14 See Pitman B. Potter, *China's Peripheries: The Capacity for Control* (forthcoming).

15 Jay Dautcher, 'Reading out-of-print: popular culture and protest in China's western frontier,' in Timothy B. Weston and Lionel M. Jenson (eds), *China Beyond the Headlines*, Lanham, MD: Rowman & Littlefield, 2000, pp. 273–94.

16 He Baogang and Barry Sautman, 'The Dalai Lama's Tibet initiative,' *Pacific Affairs*, 79(4), Winter 2005/06.

17 Robert Marquand, 'Hong Kong democrat speaks,' *Christian Science Monitor*, 21 July 2006, p. 5.

18 Guoguang Wu, 'Passions, politics, and politicians: Beijing between Taipei and Washington,' *Pacific Review*, 17(2), June 2004, pp. 179–98.

19 Elizabeth Economy and Michael Oksenberg (eds), *China Joins the World: Progress and Prospects*, NY: Council on Foreign Relations Press, 1999; David Shambaugh (ed.), *Powershift: China and Asia's New Dynamics*, Berkeley: University of California Press, 2006.

20 David M. Lampton, *Same Bed, Different Dreams: Managing U.S.–China Relations, 1989–2000*, Berkeley: University of California Press, 2002.

21 Judith F. Kornberg and John R. Faust, *China in World Politics: Policies, Processes, Prospects*, 2nd edn, Vancouver, BC: University of British Columbia Press, 2005.

22 Brantly Womack, 'China and Southeast Asia: asymmetry, leadership, and normalcy,' *Pacific Affairs*, 76(4), Winter 2003/04, pp. 529–48.

23 Juan Lindau and Timothy Cheek (eds), *Market Reform and Political Change: Comparing China and Mexico*, Lanham, MD: Rowman & Littlefield, 1997.

24 Peter Singlemann, 'Institutional democratization: changing political practices and the sugarcane growers' Union of the PRI,' in Gerardo Otero (ed.), *Mexico in Transition: Neoliberal Globalism, the State and Civil Society*, London: Zed Books, 2004, pp. 89–103.

Conclusion

1 Murray A. Rubinstein (ed.), *Taiwan: A New History*, Armonk, NY: M. E. Sharpe, 1999, pp. 292–6.

Suggested reading

Useful textbooks

Fairbank, John King and Merle Goldman, *China: A New History*, 2nd edn, Cambridge, MA: Harvard University Press, 2006

Saich, Tony, *Governance and Politics of China*, London: Palgrave, 2001

Spence, Jonathan, *In Search of Modern China*, New York: W. W. Norton, 1999

Good collections of articles, including further suggested reading on specific topics

Blum, Susan Debra and Lionel M. Jensen (eds), *China Off Center: Mapping the Margins of the Middle Kingdom*, Honolulu: University of Hawaii Press, 2002

Perry, Elizabeth J. and Mark Selden (eds), *Chinese Society: Change, Conflict and Resistance*, 2nd edn, London: Routledge, 2003

Weston, Timothy B. and Lionel M. Jensen (eds), *China's Transformations: The Stories Beyond the Headlines*, Lanham, MD: Rowman & Littlefield, 2006

Chinese voices – translations from Chinese intellectuals (Wang) and ordinary people (Ye), and activists (Chen and Wu)

Wang, Chaohua (ed.), *One China, Many Paths*, London: Verso, 2003

Ye, Sang, *China Candid: The People's Republic*, ed. Geremie R. Barmé with Miriam Lang, Berkeley: University of California Press, 2005

Chen, Guidi and Wu Chunto, *Will the Boat Sink the Water? The Life of China's Peasants*, NY: Public Affairs, 2006

Well-researched and readable academic studies of key topics

Fewsmith, Joseph, *China since Tiananmen: The Politics of Transition*, New York: Cambridge University Press, 2001

Friedmann, John, *China's Urban Transition*, Minneapolis: University of Minnesota Press, 2005

Gladney, Dru C., *Dislocating China: Muslims, Minorities and Other Subaltern Subjects*, Chicago, IL: University of Chicago Press, 2004

Goldman, Merle, *From Comrade to Citizen: The Struggle for Political Rights in China*, Cambridge, MA: Harvard University Press, 2005

Lee, Ching Kwan, *Gender and the South China Miracle: Two Worlds of Factory Women*, Berkeley: University of California Press, 1998

Madsen, Richard, *China and the American Dream: A Moral Inquiry*, Berkeley: University of California Press, 1995

O'Brien, Kevin J. and Li Lianjiang, *Rightful Resistance in Rural China*, New York: Cambridge University Press, 2006

Shambaugh, David (ed.), *Powershift: China and Asia's New Dynamics*, Berkeley: University of California Press, 2006

Zhao, Suisheng, *A Nation-State by Construction: Dynamics of Modern Chinese Nationalism*, Stanford, CA: Stanford University Press, 2004

Index